The Genealogist's **U.S. History** Pocket Reference

Quick Facts & **Timelines** of **American History** to Help Understand Your Ancestors

by Nancy Hendrickson

FAMILY TREE BOOKS
CINCINNATI, OHIO
shopfamilytree.com

Contents

Introduction

Genealogists acquire many skills throughout their research, among them the unofficial title "historian." That's because it oftentimes takes a knowledge of historical events, places or people to unlock family tree puzzles.

From one census to another, ancestors seemingly disappear off the face of the earth. But in studying the history of a specific time or place, genealogists learn to map well-known migrations, trace early pandemics and follow the trail of military upheaval—each of which could have sent the family moving from one place to another.

To help in your family tree research, we've compiled key resources in American history—from political and military battles to popular books, famous people, maps, immigration statistics and favorite foods. You'll find it all in an easy-to-read format that spans six eras, from colonial America to 1945. Keep this guide in your pocket or bag as a quick reference to the most significant events in the country's past.

How to Use This Book

Check the table of contents of this book to familiarize yourself with the information inside it. When you're trying to find an ancestor in a specific era, consult the chapter on that era. The events of the era may have directly impacted your ancestor. Wars create service records for soliders, but also may have displaced your ancestors if fighting took place on their land. Disasters and disease also displace people. Additionally, you'll find listings of censuses taken during the time period. Search these census records in online databases, such as subscription site Ancestry.com **<ancestry.com>** or free site FamilySearch **<familysearch.org>**.

1

Colonial America to **1763**

About the Era

The late 16th and early 17th centuries were an era of seagoing exploration. Men whose names now fill history books were among the first Europeans to set foot upon the North American continent: Hudson, Coronado, de Soto, La Salle, Joliet, Raleigh, Drake and Marquette. While the Spanish sought gold, the French and Dutch were eager to build a fur trade empire. The English, alone, sought a New World where colonies could be established based on religious tolerance.

America Before the Europeans

More than 10,000 years ago, America was settled by indigenous peoples crossing the land bridge from northeast Asia. They were primarily nomads, hunters and foragers.

One of the greatest cultures to arise was the Anasazi. Many of their cliff dwellings in the southwest still stand, with the most famous being Mesa Verde in present-day Colorado.

On the eastern part of the continent, Native Americans known as the Mound Builders constructed earthworks that were probably burial mounds or temples. These people lived on the eastern edge of the great prairies. Mound Builders were comprised of two groups: Woodland and Mississippian.

Woodland mounds were built as late as the 18th century, with the most noted in southern Ohio, built by the Hopewell culture. The Mississippians began mound building about 700 C.E. in the central and lower Mississippi River. The Cahokia Mounds in Illinois (near St. Louis) are the best known remnants of this culture.

Exploring the Continent

EXPLORER	DATE	PLACE
Leif Eriksson	1000 C.E.	Baffin Island
Christopher Columbus	1492	Caribbean
John Cabot	1497	Coast of Maine
Sebastian Cabot	1508	Hudson Bay
Ponce de Leon	1513	Florida
Jacques Cartier	1535	St. Lawrence River
Hernando de Soto	1539	Florida
Francisco Vásquez de Coronado	1541	New Mexico to Kansas
Juan Rodríguez Cabrillo	1542	California Coast
Sir Francis Drake	1579	Central California Coast
Sir Walter Raleigh	1584	Virginia
Don Juan de Oñate	1605	Texas, New Mexico
Henry Hudson	1609	Delaware Bay
René-Robert Cavelier also called Robert de La Salle	1684	Texas Coast

★ **TRIVIA** ★ Amerigo Vespucci coined the phrase *Mundus Novus*—New World. German cartographer Martin Waldseemuller used Vespucci's first name to label the new region.

First Settlements in America

DATE	FIRST SETTLEMENT
1607	Jamestown
1620	Plymouth
1630	Boston
1634	St. Mary's
1635	Hartford
1636	Providence

Formation of the Original 13 Colonies

COLONY	FORMATION	FOUNDED BY
Virginia	1607	London Company
Massachusetts	1620	Puritans
New Hampshire	1623	John Mason
Maryland	1634	Lord Baltimore
Connecticut	1635	Thomas Hooker
Rhode Island	1636	Roger Williams
Delaware	1638	New Sweden Company
North Carolina	1653	Virginians
South Carolina	1663	Nobles with a Royal Charter
New Jersey	1664	Lord Berkeley and Sir George Carteret
New York	1664	Duke of York
Pennsylvania	1682	William Penn
Georgia	1732	James Oglethorpe

Important Documents of the Era

FIRST VIRGINIA CHARTER, 1606: A document from King James I to the Virginia Company assigning land rights to colonists for the purpose of propagating the Christian religion.

MAYFLOWER COMPACT, 1620: First governing document of Plymouth Colony, made between the Separatists (seeking religious freedom) and the Strangers (seeking commercial gain).

CHARTER OF MASSACHUSETTS BAY, 1629: Royal Charter granted to the New England Company, whose goal was to change the emphasis of the colony from trade to religion.

FUNDAMENTAL ORDERS OF CONNECTICUT, 1639: Established the basics of government in Connecticut.

CONNECTICUT COLONY CHARTER, 1662: Royal charter granted to the colony by King Charles II.

FIRST THANKSGIVING PROCLAMATION: June 20, 1676.

GREAT LAW OF PENNSYLVANIA, 1682: Imprisonment for debt was eliminated, death sentence abolished except for treason and murder.

THE ALBANY PLAN, 1754: Proposed by Benjamin Franklin at the Albany Congress, it was an early attempt at forming a union of the colonies "under one government as far as might be necessary for defense and other general important purposes" during the French and Indian War.

Events That Shaped the Era

1584 Sir Walter Raleigh discovers Virginia

1587 Sir Walter Raleigh sends 117 people to Roanoke Island, off the coast of North Carolina

1590 Roanoke settlers vanish, leaving the word *croatoan* carved into a tree

1599 Acoma Massacre in New Mexico

1607 Settlers arrive at Jamestown

1613 Dutch fur traders arrive on Manhattan Island

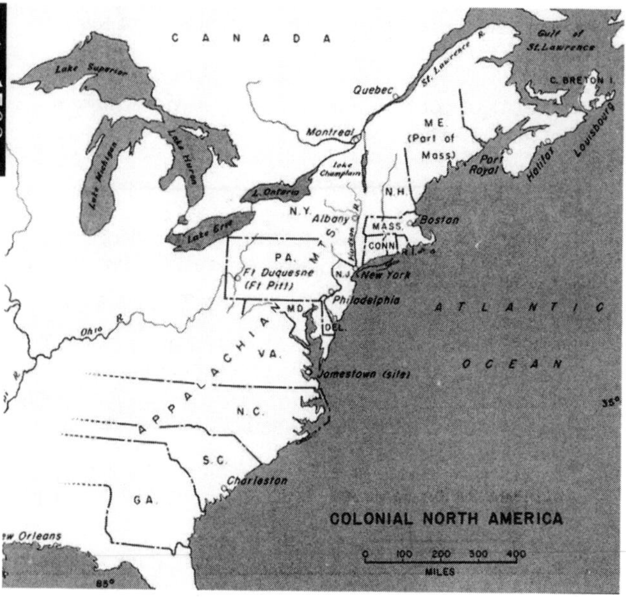

Colonial America 1689–1783
Courtesy of the University of Texas Libraries, The University of Texas at Austin

1619 Dutch traders import African slaves at the request of Virginia tobacco planters

House of Burgesses established

1624 Virginia becomes a royal colony

1630 Puritans found Massachusetts Bay Colony

1634 Maryland settled

1640s Five Iroquois Nations go to war over fur trade

1651 First Navigation Act passed (restricted trade with the Dutch)

1659 Quakers executed in Boston

1663 Carolina proprietorship granted

1673 Marquette and Joliet explore Mississippi

1681 La Salle claims Louisiana for France

1682 William Penn founds Pennsylvania

1688 Antislavery protests in America

1692 Salem witchcraft trials

1699 Wool Act (restricted trade on textiles)

1704 Attack on Deerfield, Mass., by French and Indians

1705 Slavery defined in Virginia (Virginia Slave Code)

1713 Treaty of Utrecht (in part, ended French-backed Indian attacks)

1718 Spanish mission established along San Antonio River in Texas

1733 Molasses Act (imposed a tax on colonists who imported molasses from non-British colonies)

Slaves offered freedom in Spanish Florida

1734 Great Awakening (A wave for religious revival that began in New England, ignited by Jonathan Edwards)

1747 First issue of Benjamin Franklin's *Poor Richard's Almanack*

1747-1748 Record snowfalls in much of the United States

1750 Iron Act (sought to restrict manufacturing in the Colonies)

1751 Currency Act (sought to regulate paper money issued by the colonies)

1760 Slaves comprise 20 percent of American population

The Puebloan Revolution

After long-lasting conflict between Pueblo peoples and the Spanish, a coordinated uprising took place in 1680, at dozens of settlements in the Southwest. Indians destroyed buildings and churches, killing more than 400 Spaniards. Santa Fe was burned, driving the Spanish back to El Paso.

This was the first instance of native peoples working together to drive out Spanish colonists. The Spanish worked for more than 20 years to reassert control over the Rio Grande Pueblos, but were unsuccessful. During the winter of 1700, the Hopi sacked a church at Awatovi, killing the men and kidnapping the women and children.

The Witchcraft Trials

The Salem witchcraft trials were a series of hearings and prosecutions of people accused of witchcraft in colonial Massachusetts. On May 27, 1692, a special Court of Oyer and Terminer was established to hear the cases.

The first, that of Bridget Bishop, alleged that Bishop had employed spells and charms against several men. Once rebuffed by the men, their loved ones suffered inexplicable injury. On June 10, Bishop became the first of 19 Salem residents to hang for the crime of witchcraft. By September, the frenzy against alleged witches was so widespread that more than 100 accused witches and wizards were awaiting trial. Several residents of Massachusetts fled to New Amsterdam (New York).

Pressure from prominent religious leaders, such as Cotton Mather, caused Governor Phipps to dissolve the Court in late October. The last three people tried were pardoned in May 1693. On December 17, 1696, the General Court adopted a resolution calling for a day of fasting and repentance for the trials.

Wars of the Era

THE PEQUOT WAR, 1634–1638: Pequot tribe against an alliance of the Massachusetts Bay, Plymouth, and Saybrook colonies. Culmination of a series of economic and territorial conflicts.

OPECHANCANOUGH VS. VIRGINIA COLONISTS, 1664: Opechancanough launched an assault on English colonists in Virginia. At least 400 colonists were killed.

BATTLE FOR NEW NETHERLAND, 1664: Dutch leader Peter Stuyvesant lost New Netherland (New York) to England in the Second Anglo-Dutch War.

KING PHILIP'S WAR, 1675: Began as a result of English pressures to control Native Americans in New England. "Philip" (the Wampanoag leader named Metacomet or Metacom) was drawn and quartered and his followers sold into slavery.

BACON'S REBELLION, 1676: Virginia settlers, led by Nathaniel Bacon, rebelled against government policy toward Indians and successfully attacked Indian settlements.

KING WILLIAM'S WAR, 1689: The first of the French and Indian Wars, this war grew out of a European conflict. French and Americans (aided by their Indian allies) staged raids against Montreal and Quebec, New York and New England. The Treaty of Ryswick returned all territory to pre-war status.

LEISLER'S REBELLION, 1689: After James II was overthrown in England, colonists removed royal governors in several colonies. Led by Jacob Leisler, who became governor of New York.

QUEEN ANNE'S WAR, 1702: English colonists in the Carolinas attacked Spanish territory in Florida in an attempt to seize the fort at St. Augustine. French Canadians raided English settlements in New England and English colonists invaded Quebec. This conflict was called the Abnaki War in Maine, where French Canadians gathered Abnakis who attacked English settlements in Maine.

TUSCARORA, 1711: Tuscarora Indians attacked white settlers in retaliation for white raids on Tuscarora villages.

STONO REBELLION, 1739: South Carolina slaves rebel, killing whites and urging other slaves to join them.

FRENCH AND INDIAN WAR, 1754: In Europe, known as the Seven Years' War. Major conflict related to territory. The British wanted to take over French-held lands in America as well as the fur trade. The war ended in 1763, with the Treaty of Paris.

PONTIAC'S REBELLION, 1763: Pontiac, an Ottawa Indian chief, led an attack on Detroit. The conflict ended when the Indians failed to receive French aid.

Inventions

DATE	INVENTION
1659	Horse-drawn water pump
1712	Automated water pump
1714	Mercury thermometer with temperature scale
1717	Swim fins
1730	Octant
1742	Franklin Stove
1749	Lightning rod
1752	Flexible urinary catheter
1761	Harmonica

Famous People of the Era

CAPTAIN JOHN SMITH (1580-1631): One of the leaders at Jamestown

POWHATAN (WAHUNSONACOCK): The main political and military power facing the early colonists; father of Pocahontas

POCAHONTAS (c. 1595-1617) : Aided Jamestown colonists; later married tobacco planter John Rolfe

SQUANTO (B. CIRCA 1580): Aided the Plymouth colonists by teaching them native methods of growing corn

JOHN CARVER (1576-1621): First governor of Plymouth Colony

WILLIAM BRADFORD (1590-1657): Governor of Plymouth Colony and its chief historian

WILLIAM BREWSTER (1566-1644): Pilgrim leader and preacher, arrived on the *Mayflower*

EDWARD WINSLOW (1595-1655): Diplomat who negotiated treaty with Massasoit and established fur trading

MYLES STANDISH (1584-1656): Professional soldier, military advisor for the Plymouth Colony

WILLIAM PENN (1644-1718): Founder of Pennsylvania, noted for championing democracy and religious freedom

GEN. EDWARD BRADDOCK (1695-1755): Commander-in-chief for the 13 Colonies during the time of the French and Indian War

GEORGE WASHINGTON (1732-1799): Senior American aide to Gen. Braddock during the French and Indian War

BENJAMIN FRANKLIN (1706-1790): American author (*Poor Richard's Almanack*) and inventor

English Monarchs in America's Early Colonization

MONARCH	REIGN	FAMILY
Charles II	1660-1685	Stuart
James II	1685-1688	Stuart
Mary II and William III	1689-1694/1689-1702	Stuart/House of Orange
Anne	1702-1714	Stuart
George I	1714-1727	House of Hanover
George II	1727-1760	House of Hanover

Social Classes in Virginia

FIELD HANDS: African slaves, working primarily in tobacco fields; work was from sunup to sundown with Sunday off

HOUSE SERVANTS: African slaves who worked in the household as cooks, laundresses, manservants, blacksmiths, coopers or other skilled jobs

FREE BLACKS: A small part of the population; could own property but did not have all the rights of whites

FARMERS: Worked small farms with the aid of family members and possibly one to two slaves

MIDDLING: Colonial version of the middle class; worked in trades such as blacksmithing, silversmithing and printing; were also in professional occupations such as merchants, lawyers and doctors

GENTRY: The top of the colonial social structure; they were the wealthiest, owned large tracts of land and served in local government

---

★ **TRIVIA** ★ Women typically married in their late teens or early twenties and bore children every two years throughout their child-bearing years. Families averaged between six and eight children.

Life Expectancy 1640–1700 (For a Person Aged 20)

FOR WOMEN	FOR MEN	LOCATION
39	48	Middlesex County, Virginia
62	64	Andover, Massachusetts Bay Colony
62	69	Plymouth Colony

Mortality

Half of all Europeans who settled in America before 1640 died within their first year in America. A quarter of all children born in the colonies before 1640 died before reaching age one. During this time, half of all marriages ended in the death of one partner before the couple's seventh wedding anniversary.

In Virginia, the prevalent diseases in the 17th century were smallpox, plague, beriberi, malaria and yellow fever. The prevailing diseases in New England were said to be typhoid fever, tuberculosis, pneumonia and scurvy.

In 1610, 338 out of 398 colonists of Jamestown died; in 1621, half the population of Massachusetts perished.

The high mortality rate was largely due to epidemics, which were usually introduced by ships' crews at seaports and which then swept through the colonies, decimating the colonists and, to an even greater extent, the American Indians. The predominating epidemics of the 17th century were smallpox and measles; that of the 18th century, yellow fever.

The smallpox epidemics were finally controlled by inoculation of smallpox virus from active cases, although the practice was opposed by the public. In a smallpox epidemic in 1721, the Reverend Cotton Mather successfully, but secretly, inoculated his own son.

Medical Treatments

For bloodletting:
"Make your incision large and not too deepe,
That bloud have speedy issue with the fume
So that from sinewes you all hurt do keepe,
Nor may you (as I toucht before) presume
In sixe ensuing houres at all to sleep."
From Regimen Salerni

For Hair Loss:

"Take a good number of bees that be labouring to make honey, dry them and make them to powder. Then be put in common oyle and mingle them together and with ointment anoint the place you will have hair and certainly it will come without pain."
From Natura Exenterata

Epidemics

DISEASE	YEAR	PLACE
Smallpox	1617-1619	Massachusetts Bay Colony
Smallpox	1633	Plymouth Colony
Measles	1657	Boston
Yellow Fever	1690	New York City
Measles	1713-1715	New England
Smallpox	1721-1722	Boston
Measles	1729	Boston
Influenza	1732	All colonies
Yellow Fever	1737	Virginia
Smallpox	1738	South Carolina
Measles	1739-1740	Boston
Measles	1747	Connecticut, New York, Pennsylvania, South Carolina

Books of the Era

- *A True Relation of Such Occurrences and Accidents of Noate as Hath Happened in Virginia* by Captain John Smith, 1608
- *Introduction to the Devout Life* by St. Francis de Sales, 1609
- *The Generall Historie of Virginia, New England, and the Summer Isles* by Captain John Smith, 1624
- *History of Plymouth Plantation, 1620-47* by William Bradford, 1647

- *Exposition of the Creed* by John Pearson, 1659
- *An Essay Concerning Human Understanding* by John Locke, 1690
- *The London Spy* by Ned Ward, 1703
- *Robinson Crusoe* by Daniel Defoe, 1719
- *Moll Flanders* by Daniel Defoe, 1722
- *Gulliver's Travels* by Jonathan Swift, 1726
- *The History of Tom Jones* by Henry Fielding, 1749
- *Candide* by Voltaire, 1759
- *The Life and Opinions of Tristram Shandy* by Laurence Sterne, 1759

★ **TRIVIA** ★ In 1650, Anne Bradstreet became the first female poet ever published in both England and America, with her book of poetry, *The Tenth Muse Lately Sprung Up in America.*

Colonial Colleges

YEAR	COLLEGE
1636	Harvard
1693	William and Mary
1701	Yale
1746	College of New Jersey (Princeton)
1754	King's (Columbia)
1755	College of Philadelphia (University of Pennsylvania)

Songs Of The Era

- "Barbara Allen"
- "The Bold Soldier"
- "Death of Wolfe"
- "The Deceived Maid"

- "The Girl I Left Behind Me"
- "Greensleeves"
- "The Nightingale"
- "Silkie"

Popular Foods of the Era

- Apple Tansey
- Carolina Fish Muddle
- Pennsylvania Dutch Apple Dumplings
- Welsh Rabbit
- Tidewater Chili
- Fish House Punch
- Yankee Codfish in Gravy
- Flummery
- Hasty Pudding

Recipe From the Era

Thomas Jefferson's Catfish Soup

5 whole(s) (1 ¼ pounds each) catfish or other mild fish, cleaned
1 slice(s) (½-inch-thick) ham
2 small yellow onions, finely chopped
3 sprig(s) parsley
1 sprig(s) marjoram
2 sprig(s) tarragon
3 sprig(s) chervil
6 whole(s) black peppercorns
1 teaspoon(s) salt
1 cup(s) heavy cream
2 egg yolks
2 tablespoon(s) finely minced parsley

Beurre Manié:
3 tablespoon(s) flour
2 tablespoon(s) butter

Directions:
Coarsely chop four of the catfish. Place in a large saucepan with the ham, chopped onions, herbs, peppercorns, salt and two quarts of water. Bring to a boil and simmer 30 minutes. Pass through a food mill into a clean saucepan. Fillet the remaining catfish and cut the fillets into bite-sized pieces. Reserve. Make the beurre manié: Knead the butter and flour together until combined. Just prior to serving, return the fish broth to the stove and add the fish fillets. Bring just to the simmer and cook gently for one minute. Add the heavy cream and the beurre manié and simmer briefly. Turn the heat off under the soup. Meanwhile, break up the egg yolks in a separate bowl. Temper the yolks by adding slowly two cups of the soup to the yolks in the bowl, stirring the yolks constantly, and then returning the yolk mixture to the soup. Serve immediately, garnished with the minced parsley.

Most Popular Names

MALE	FEMALE
John	Abigail
William	Susanna
Edward	Mary
Richard	Elizabeth
Thomas	Sarah
Samuel	Hannah
Joseph	Rebecca
	Ruth
	Anne
	Martha

Colonial Churches

DENOMINATION	NUMBER OF CHURCHES IN 1700	NUMBER OF CHURCHES IN 1740
Anglican	111	246
Baptist	33	96
Congregational (attended by Puritans)	146	423
Dutch Reformed	26	78
German Reformed	0	51
Lutheran	7	95
Presbyterian	28	160
Catholic	22	27

Population in the 13 Colonies

YEAR	POPULATION
1625	1,980
1641	50,000
1688	200,000
1700	250,888
1710	331,711
1720	466,185
1730	629,445
1740	905,563
1750	1,107,676
1760	1,593,625

Population Percentages

New England (MA, NH, RI, CT)	27%
Middle Colonies (NY, NJ, PA, DE)	25.9%
South (MD, VA, NC, SC, GA)	47.1%

Immigration

Between 1700 and 1775 more than 300,000 Europeans migrated to America. The two largest immigrant groups, after the English were:

Scots-Irish (approximately 200,000)
This ethnic group settled in the middle colonies, especially in Pennsylvania, because Philadelphia was a major port. Subsequently, the Scots-Irish migrated south following the Great Philadelphia Wagon Road, the main road used for settling the interior southern colonies. Traveling down the Shenandoah Valley, they then went into Virginia and the Carolinas.

Germans (approximately 85,000)
German immigration was first encouraged by William Penn. The Germans settled close to Philadelphia in 1683. Another group of Germans settled in New York's Hudson Valley around 1708, and in Virginia around 1712. By the time of the Revolution, Germans had settled all along the eastern seaboard.

Slaves as a Percentage of the Population

YEAR	NEW ENGLAND	MIDDLE COLONIES	CHESAPEAKE	LOWER SOUTH	TOTAL
1700	2%	7%	22%	17%	11%
1730	3%	8%	23%	43%	14%

The single largest group coming to America were African slaves. The first slaves arrived in 1619. During the 18th century, importation of slaves increased as planters sought a cheap alternative to indentured servants. Nearly 280,000 Africans were forcibly transported to North America during this time period.

The Economy and the Triangle Trade

The so-called Triangle Trade took place between America, Africa and England. Ships left England with trade goods, then sailed to Africa where they traded goods for slaves. The ships then transported the slaves to the West Indies or the Colonies where they were exchanged for sugar, tobacco and rice. The trade ships then sailed back to England with the produce, often stopping at New England ports to sell sugar, which was used to make rum.

The death rate among slaves on board the ships could run as high as 50 percent. Dehydration, caused by lack of drinking water and high loss of bodily fluids from fevers or dysentery, was a primary killer aboard the ships.

Slaves were confined below deck in cargo holds on two tiers of shelves with only about 18-inches between the shelves.

A 25-year-old male slave could sell for as much as $800. Prices rose through puberty as productivity and experience increased. In 19th-century New Orleans, prices peaked at about age 22 for females and age 25 for males.

Colonial and Territorial Censuses of the Era

ALABAMA: 1706–1819 (various years)

DELAWARE: 1671, 1782

LOUISIANA: 1699, 1700, 1706, 1711, 1721, 1722, 1724, 1725, 1726, 1727, 1731, 1732

MICHIGAN: 1710

NEW HAMPSHIRE: 1732, 1744

NEW MEXICO: 1600; 1750-1845 (various years and areas)

NEW YORK: 1693; 1700 (militia)

PENNSYLVANIA: 1680 (residents along the Delaware River)

RHODE ISLAND: 1730 (fragments); 1740-1743, 1747

VIRGINIA: 1624, 1625

2

Revolutionary America 1763 to 1783

1763–1783

About the Era

In the decade before the American Revolution, Britain began a series of legislative acts that restricted trade, raised taxes and strictly regulated colonial currency. Due to the high cost of the French and Indian War as well as maintaining a garrison force in America (£200,000 per year), the British government felt that the colonists should bear part of the financial burden. One source of revenue was to tax imports and exports via the Navigation Acts, a series of acts that required Americans to export goods only to British ports and only on British ships.

In 1763, the British government began a more aggressive tax policy beginning with a revised Sugar Act. Under the new terms, sugar, wine, silk, calico and coffee imported from non-British colonies would be subject to an increased duty. Soon thereafter, in 1764, the Currency Act forbade the Colonies from issuing paper money, making it even more difficult to pay the new customs duties.

In 1774, a series of laws known as the Intolerable Acts were passed by Parliament. Four of them were issued in direct response to the Boston Tea Party of 1773. Many colonists saw the acts as a violation of their rights, and in September of 1774 the First Continental Congress met in Philadelphia. The stage was set for Revolution.

Events That Shaped the Era

1764 Sugar Act, Currency Act

Benjamin Franklin suggests American representation in Parliament

1765 Stamp Act, Quartering Act

Riots by Sons of Liberty

1766 Stamp Act repealed

1767 Townshend Acts

Daughters of Liberty make homespun cloth

1768 Circular letter adopted in Massachusetts

British Army occupies Boston

1770 Boston Massacre

1772 Patriots burn the British customs schooner *Gaspee*

1773 Tea Act, Boston Tea Party

1774 Minutemen established

Intolerable Acts (Coercive Acts) punish Massachusetts

First Continental Congress, 56 delegates from all colonies except Georgia

1775 Battles of Lexington and Concord

Second Continental Congress

Paul Revere's "midnight ride"

Battle of Bunker Hill

Siege of Boston

George Washington assumed command of the 17,000 man Army

1776 Thomas Paine's *Common Sense* is published

Declaration of Independence

Howe defeats Washington in New York

American victories at Trenton and Princeton

Territorial Growth 1775.
Courtesy of the University of Texas Libraries, The University of Texas at Austin

1777 British occupy Philadelphia

Slavery abolished in Vermont

British defeated at Saratoga

Continental Army suffers the winter at Valley Forge

1778 British capture Savannah

1779 General John Sullivan attacks the British-allied Iroquois nations

Spain declares war on England

1780 British capture Charleston

American army wins at King's Mountain

1781 Lord Cornwallis invades Virginia

Cornwallis surrenders at Yorktown

1783 Treaty of Paris

Newburgh Conspiracy (Continental officers threaten to revolt due to Congress' non-payment for their Army services)

British leave New York

★ **TRIVIA** ★ **It's reported that when Lord Cornwallis surrendered his nearly 9,000 men at the Siege of Yorktown, the British band played the tune, "The World Turned Upside Down."**

British Legislation That Spurred the Revolution

1764 SUGAR ACT: Placed new duties on importation of sugar and other commodities.

1764 CURRENCY ACT: Regulated the ability of colonies to print paper money.

1765 STAMP ACT: Required that every paper document bear a revenue stamp; this included everything from newspapers to playing cards. The Sons of Liberty rioted in response to this act.

1766 DECLARATORY ACT: Affirmed Parliament's authority to pass laws for the colonies.

1767 TOWNSHEND ACTS: Levied duties on glass, lead, paint and tea; allowed blanket search warrants and jury-less courts; colonists respond by harassing British merchants.

1773 TEA ACT: Brought widespread resistance leading to the Boston Tea Party.

1774 IMPARTIAL ADMINISTRATION OF JUSTICE ACT: Allowed the royal governor of a colony to move trials to other colonies or even to England if he feared that juries in those colonies wouldn't judge a case fairly.

1774 MASSACHUSETTS GOVERNMENT ACT: Made all law officers subject to appointment by the royal governor; all town meetings were banned if they didn't have the approval of the royal governor.

1774 BOSTON PORT ACT: Closed the port of Boston until the price of the dumped tea was recovered; made Salem the new capital and Marblehead the official port of entry.

1774 QUARTERING ACT: Allowed royal troops to stay in houses or empty buildings if barracks were not available.

1774 THE QUEBEC ACT: Removed the fur trade between the Ohio and Mississippi Rivers from colonial jurisdiction and into the hands of the province of Quebec.

★ TRIVIA ★ On December 16, 1773, the Sons of Liberty, disguised as Mohawks, emptied 342 chests of tea valued at £18,000 into Boston Harbor. This event became known as the Boston Tea Party.

Boston Massacre

On March 5, 1770, British soldiers killed five men who were harassing a British sentry. The soldiers fired into the crowd, instantly killing three people and wounding others, two of whom would die of their wounds. A free black man, Crispus Attucks, was the first to be killed. Eight soldiers, one officer and four civilians were arrested and charged with murder. The accused were defended by John Adams. Six soldiers were acquitted and two convicted of manslaughter. This event was a preamble to all-out war. Boston marked the anniversary of the massacre as Massacre Day until American independence was recognized in 1783.

Major Battles of the American Revolution (1775–1783)

DATE	NAME	PLACE	VICTOR
April 19, 1775	The Battles of Lexington and Concord	Lexington and Concord, Massachusetts	Colonials
May 10, 1775	The Siege of Fort Ticonderoga	Fort Ticonderoga, New York	Colonials
June 16, 1775	The Battle of Bunker (Breeds) Hill	Charlestown, Massachusetts	British
December 31, 1775	The Battle of Quebec	Quebec City, Province of Quebec	British
August 27, 1776	The Battle of Long Island (Brooklyn Heights)	Long Island, New York	British
October 28, 1776	The Battle of White Plains	White Plains, New York	British
December 26, 1776	The Battle of Trenton	Trenton, New Jersey	Colonials
January 3, 1777	The Battle of Princeton	Princeton, New Jersey	Colonials
August 16, 1777	The Battle of Bennington	Bennington, New York	Colonials
September 11, 1777	The Battle of Brandywine	Near Chadds Ford, Pennsylvania	British
September 19, 1777	The Battle of Saratoga (Freeman's Farm)	Saratoga County, New York	Colonials
October 4, 1777	The Battle of Germantown	Germantown, Pennsylvania	British
October 7, 1777	The Battle of Saratoga (Bemis Heights)	Saratoga County, New York	Colonials
June 28, 1778	The Battle of Monmouth	Monmouth, New Jersey	Draw
December 29, 1778	The Capture of Savannah	Savannah, Georgia	British

DATE	NAME	PLACE	VICTOR
March 29, 1780	The Siege of Charleston	Charleston, South Carolina	British
August 16, 1780	The Battle of Camden	North of Camden, South Carolina	British
October 7, 1780	The Battle of King's Mountain	Near Blackburn, S.C. and King's Mountain, N.C.	Colonials
January 17, 1781	The Battle of Cowpens	Cowpens, South Carolina	Colonials
March 15, 1781	The Battle of Guilford Courthouse	Guilford Courthouse, North Carolina	British
October 9, 1781	The Battle of Yorktown	Yorktown, Virginia	British surrender

"The Fort That Saved America"

Fort Mifflin is located on the Delaware River on the outskirts of Philadelphia. For six weeks, in the fall of 1777, soldiers at Fort Mifflin were able to halt British naval attempts to resupply their occupying forces in Philadelphia. Early in November, Mifflin underwent the largest bombardment of the entire Revolution. It's reported that in one hour, 1,000 cannon balls were fired at the fort. Mifflin's defenders were forced to evacuate on November 15, but their delaying tactics gave Washington the time he needed to get the army safely to Valley Forge.

Revolutionary War Casualties (Estimates)

ALLIANCE	DEATHS
Patriot	25,000
British	19,640
German	6,354

★ **TRIVIA** ★ Philadelphia, with a population of 30,000, was the largest city during the American Revolution.

Military Leaders

GEORGE WASHINGTON (1732-1799): Veteran of the French and Indian War, wealthy Virginia planter; responsible for holding together a poorly equipped and poorly trained volunteer army.

BENEDICT ARNOLD (1741-1801): General who commanded the fort at West Point; changed allegiance and became a brigadier general in the British Army.

GEORGE ROGERS CLARK (1752-1818): Responsible for the capture of Kaskaskia and Vincennes, which weakened British influence in the Northwest Territory; Brother of William Clark (Lewis and Clark Expedition).

ETHAN ALLEN (1738-1789): Leader of the Green Mountain Boys and responsible for the capture of Fort Ticonderoga; a founder of the state of Vermont.

MAJ. JOHN ANDRÉ (1750-1780): British Army officer who worked with Benedict Arnold to turn over the plans to West Point; was captured and hanged as a spy.

GEN. SIR HENRY CLINTON (1730-1795): Second British commander-in-chief of North America.

LORD CHARLES CORNWALLIS (1738-1805): Leader in the British "Southern Strategy," served under Gen. William Howe and Henry Clinton; surrendered to Washington on October 19, 1781.

GEN. WILLIAM HOWE (1729-1814): First commander-in-chief of the British forces in America.

GEN. NATHANAEL GREENE (1742-1786): One of Washington's most trusted generals; helped rebuild the Continental Army in the South.

GEN. THOMAS GAGE (1719-1787): Involved in policies surrounding several early American conflicts, including French and Indian War, Pontiac's Rebellion and the Revolutionary War.

MAJ. GEN. CHARLES LEE (1732-1782): Veteran of the French and Indian War; was court-martialed for disobeying Washington's orders at the Battle of Monmouth.

MARQUIS DE LAFAYETTE (1757-1834): French citizen who served as a major-general in the Continental Army under George Washington; later became a leader in the French Revolution.

BARON FRIEDRICH VON STEUBEN (1730-1794): Credited with teaching the Continental Army the essentials of military drills, tactics and disciplines; served as Washington's chief-of-staff later in the war.

LT. COL. BANASTRE TARLETON (1754-1833): British solider considered a butcher by American troops; because of the atrocities he committed during the war, he was not invited to the surrender dinner given for Lord Cornwallis.

MAJ. GEN. ANTHONY WAYNE (1745-1796) "MAD ANTHONY": Aided in stopping Benedict Arnold from turning over the plans to West Point to the British; served with distinction at the Battle of Monmouth.

GEN. JOHN BURGOYNE (1722-1792) "GENTLEMAN JOHNNY": Surrendered his 5,000-man army to American forces on October 17, 1777, at Saratoga.

Civilian Leaders

JOHN ADAMS (1735-1826): Leading advocate for American independence; later became second president of the United States; died on the 50th anniversary of the signing of the Declaration of Independence.

PATRICK HENRY (1736-1799): Virginia planter and orator, best known for his "give me liberty or give me death" speech; later became governor of Virginia.

BENJAMIN FRANKLIN (1706-1790): Leading American author, inventor and diplomat; one of the most influential of the Founding Fathers.

THOMAS JEFFERSON (1743-1826): Virginia planter and slave owner, leading proponent for American independence; later became first secretary of state, third U.S. president; died on the 50th anniversary of the signing of the Declaration of Independence

SAMUEL ADAMS (1722-1803): Leader of the Sons of Liberty; his 1768 Circular Letter argued that the Townshend Acts were unconstitutional.

JOHN HANCOCK (1737-1793): Wealthy merchant, president of the Continental Congress; became governor of Massachusetts.

RICHARD HENRY LEE (1732-1794): Wealthy Virginia planter, introduced the motion in the Second Continental Congress calling for American independence.

Florida During the Revolution

In 1763, in exchange for Havana, Cuba, the British gained control of Florida from Spain. The British then split the area into East and West Florida, with the capitals at St. Augustine and Pensacola. The Apalachicola River was the boundary line between the two

Floridas. Both Floridas remained loyal to Great Britain during the Revolutionary War. However, Spain entered the war as an American ally and captured Pensacola in 1781. At the close of the war, Spain once again regained control of Florida.

The Mission Era in California

While the settlers on the East Coast were preparing for revolution, the Spanish were solidifying their foothold in California. Beginning in 1769, 21 Franciscan missions were built in California, all linked by El Camino Real.

DATE	MISSION	FOUNDER
1769	San Diego de Alcalà	Fr. Junípero Serra
1770	San Carlos Borromeo de Carmelo	Fr. Junípero Serra
1771	San Antonio de Padua	Fr. Junípero Serra
1771	San Gabriel Arcángel	Frs. Cambon & Somera
1772	San Luis Obispo de Tolosa	Fr. Junípero Serra
1776	San Francisco de Asís	Fr. Francisco Palóu
1776	San Juan Capistrano	Fr. Junípero Serra
1777	Santa Clara de Asís	Fr. Junípero Serra
1782	San Buenaventura	Fr. Junípero Serra
1786	Santa Barbara	Fr. Fermín Lasuén
1787	La Purísima Concepción	Fr. Fermín Lasuén
1791	Santa Cruz	Fr. Fermín Lasuén
1791	Nuestra Señora de la Soledad	Fr. Fermín Lasuén
1797	San José	Fr. Fermín Lasuén
1797	San Juan Bautista	Fr. Fermín Lasuén
1797	San Miguel Arcángel	Fr. Fermín Lasuén
1797	San Fernando Rey de España	Fr. Fermín Lasuén

DATE	MISSION	FOUNDER
1798	San Luis Rey de Francia	Fr. Fermín Lasuén
1804	Santa Inés	Fr. Estévan Tápis
1817	San Rafael Arcángel	Fr. Vicente de Sarría
1823	San Francisco Solano	Fr. José Altimíra

Between 1687 and 1711, Father Eusebio Kino established missions in northern Mexico, Baja, California and Arizona, including the famous San Xavier del Bac south of Tucson.

Europe During the Revolution

- Calcutta becomes the capital of British India
- Louis XVI becomes King of France
- Peasant revolt in Bohemia
- Jane Austen is born
- Cardinal Braschi elected as Pope Pius VI
- James Cook returns from his second voyage
- War of Bavarian Succession
- Mozart writes "Serenade in D major"
- James Cook discovers Hawaii

★ **TRIVIA** ★ **More than 100,000 copies of Thomas Paine's *Common Sense* were sold in the first three months.**

Beginning of a New Republic

In 1777, Congress passed the Articles of Confederation, making it the first national constitution. It provided for a loose confederation in which each state retained its sovereignty, freedom and independence. The Confederation had the power to declare war, make treaties, and borrow and print money. There was no executive or judicial branch and important laws had to be approved by nine of the 13 states. The Articles were not ratified by all of the states until 1781.

1763–1783

The Pox of Smallpox

By the mid-18th century smallpox was a major endemic disease everywhere in the world except in Australia. In Europe, smallpox was a leading cause of death in the 18th century, killing an estimated 400,000 Europeans each year.

In a Boston smallpox epidemic of 1776, 9,152 persons were inoculated against the disease in three days, and the total death toll for the epidemic was only 165. Following this outbreak, Gen. Washington ordered smallpox vaccinations of his entire army. This action is sometimes called the general's greatest and most important decision.

George Washington's Health

YEAR	AGE	DISEASE
1749	17	Malaria
1751	19	Smallpox
1751	19	Tuberculosis
1752	30	Malaria
1755	33	Dysentery
1757	35	Dysentery & Tuberculosis
1761	39	Malaria & Dysentery

Songs of the Era

- "American Taxation"
- "The Battle of the Kegs"
- "The British Grenadiers"
- "Castle Island Song"
- "Chester"
- "Free America"
- "Granny Wales"
- "Hail Columbia"

- "Johnny Has Gone for a Soldier"
- "The Liberty Song"
- "The Rich Lady Over the Sea"
- "The World Turned Upside Down"
- "Yankee Doodle"

Popular Foods of the Era

- Hasty Pudding
- Hoecakes
- Turtle Soup
- Gingerbread
- Bannock Cakes
- Beef, Lamb, Pork

Recipe From the Era

Indian Pudding
3 pints scalded milk
7 spoons fine Indian meal
7 eggs
½ pound raisins
4 oz. butter
spice
sugar

Directions:
Stir milk and Indian meal together while milk is still hot, let stand till cooled. Add remaining ingredients. Bake one and a half hour.

Most Popular Names

MALE	FEMALE
William	Mary
John	Elizabeth
James	Ann

MALE	FEMALE
Thomas	Sarah
Joseph	Hannah
George	Susan/Susanna
Henry	Lucy
Edward	Eliza
Richard	Martha
	Jane

Revolutionary War Land Grants

The federal government awarded bounty lands to citizens and soldiers for services rendered during the Revolution. In addition, nine state governments rewarded citizens and soldiers with bounty lands. The nine states were:

- Connecticut
- Georgia
- Maryland
- Massachusetts
- New York
- North Carolina
- Pennsylvania
- South Carolina
- Virginia

Applications for pensions or land grants may include:

- Veteran's name
- Age or birth date
- Residence
- Birthplace
- Death date and place

- Name of spouse or widow
- Marriage date and place
- Names of the children
- Ages or birth dates of the children

A 4,000-square mile tract, located in the Northwest Territory, was set aside for land warrants. This area was known as the U.S. Military District of Ohio.

Displacing of Loyalists

Between 40,000 and 50,000 Loyalists were resettled in Britain's northern colonies following the American Revolution. About 33,000 went to both Nova Scotia and New Brunswick, and about 10,000 to Quebec. Included among the settlers were 3,000 blacks who had been granted freedom in return for military service. It's estimated that when the British Army evacuated Savannah and Charleston, nearly 10,000 slaves left with them. In North Carolina and New York, estates belonging to "traitors" were confiscated. In Massachusetts, abandoned Loyalist property was handled by the courts.

Loyalist strongholds were in Georgia, New York and South Carolina, while they were at their weakest in Virginia, Maryland and Delaware.

American Population Growth

1760	1,593,625
1770	2,148.076
1780	2,780,369

Colonial and Territorial Censuses of the Era

ALABAMA: 1706–1819 (various years)

DELAWARE: 1782

FLORIDA: 1783

LOUISIANA: 1766, 1771, 1772, 1774, 1782,

MARYLAND: 1776, 1778

MICHIGAN: 1710; various through 1792 (Detroit area); 1780 (Fort St. Joseph)

MISSOURI: 1770–1804 (various areas)

NEVADA: 1776

NEW HAMPSHIRE: 1767, 1776

NEW MEXICO: 1750–1845 (various years and areas)

NEW YORK: 1774–1776

RHODE ISLAND: 1774, 1777 (men age 16 and older); 1782 (partial)

SOUTH CAROLINA: 1770 (Tryon County); 1779 (96th district); 1781 (unknown counties)

TENNESSEE: 1770–1790 (Cumberland settlements)

TEXAS: 1783 (various areas)

VIRGINIA: 1782, 1783

3

An Expanding Nation

1783 to **1830**

About the Era

During the period immediately following the Treaty of Paris, Americans were busy setting up the infrastructure of a new nation. The Constitutional Convention was tasked with writing a new constitution and in 1789, George Washington was sworn in as the first president. One of the major issues during this period was the power of the federal government versus the power of the states—an issue that would lead to a Civil War decades later.

In 1803, the young nation added 828,000 square miles to its territories via the Louisiana Purchase, opening the western frontier to a growing (and land-hungry) populace. But before a decade had passed, America was back at war with England, fighting over the impressments of American sailors and British support of Indian attacks along the frontier. Andrew Jackson's 1815 decisive Battle of New Orleans forever ended British attempts to reclaim the country. America was now ready to settle into its new role as an equal among nations.

Events That Shaped the Era

1783 Treaty of Paris signed

1786 Annapolis Convention (recommended a Constitutional Convention)

1787 Sale of first public lands directed by Congress

Constitution submitted to the States

1789 George Washington becomes first president

John Adams becomes first vice-president

1791 Bill of Rights ratified

1794 Whiskey Rebellion

1796 John Adams elected president

1797 XYZ Affair

1800 Thomas Jefferson elected president

1802 U.S. Military Academy opens at West Point, New York

1803 Marbury v. Madison rules that an act of Congress is null and void when it conflicts with provisions of the U.S. Constitution

Louisiana Purchase

1804 Beginning of Lewis and Clark Expedition

Napoleon crowns himself Emperor of the French

1807 Britain declares the slave trade illegal

1811 Battle of Tippecanoe

1812 War of 1812 begins

1814 British burn the White House

1815 Andrew Jackson wins Battle of New Orleans

1815 The Great September Gale is the first hurricane to strike New England in 180 years.

1816 Crops fail during an unseasonably cool summer in New England, called the "The Year Without a Summer," after ash from a volcanic eruption in Indonesia causes a world-wide climate shift.

1817 First Seminole War begins in Florida

1819 Florida annexed, Texas boundary defined

McCulloch v. Maryland enhances power of national government

1820 Missouri Compromise

Rural women and girls recruited as factory workers

South becomes the world's largest cotton producer

1821 Mexico gains independence from Spain with the Treaty of Córdoba

1822 American colony established in Texas

1823 Monroe Doctrine

1824 Bureau of Indian Affairs established

1825 Erie Canal completed

1828 Construction of the Baltimore and Ohio Railroad

1830 Indian Removal Act

The Treaty of Paris

Signed on September 3, 1783, by John Adams, Benjamin Franklin and John Jay, the Treaty of Paris officially ended the Revolutionary War. Among the provisions:

- Acknowledged the United States as a free, sovereign and independent country
- Established the boundaries between the U.S. and British North America

- Granted U.S. fisherman rights off the Grand Banks
- Prevention of confiscating Loyalist's property
- Release of prisoners-of-war

Under a separate agreement, Spain received East and West Floridas.

The Great Compromise

On February 21, 1787, representatives met to revise the Articles of Confederation. This meeting evolved into writing the Constitution of the United States. While all parties agreed on a form of government based on representing the people, the method of allocating votes was an unknown. Finally, the question was settled by the Connecticut Compromise, in which House members were based on population and popular vote; while the Senate would be comprised of two members from each state.

Bill of Rights

In 1791, Congress amended the Constitution to include the Bill of Rights. Among the rights were freedom of speech, religion, assembly and the press; right to bear arms and protection of quartering of troops and unreasonable search and seizure. The amendments also included a citizen's right to a trial by jury and prohibition of cruel and unusual punishment.

Order of Statehood 1787–1821

NUMBER BY ADMISSION	STATE	DATE OF ADMISSION
1	Delaware	December 7, 1787
2	Pennsylvania	December 12, 1787
3	New Jersey	December 18, 1787
4	Georgia	January 2, 1788
5	Connecticut	January 9, 1788
6	Massachusetts	February 6, 1788

NUMBER BY ADMISSION	STATE	DATE OF ADMISSION
7	Maryland	April 28, 1788
8	South Carolina	May 23, 1788
9	New Hampshire	June 21, 1788
10	Virginia	June 25, 1788
11	New York	July 26, 1788
12	North Carolina	November 21, 1789
13	Rhode Island	May 29, 1790
14	Vermont	March 4, 1791
15	Kentucky	June 1, 1792
16	Tennessee	June 1, 1796
17	Ohio	March 1, 1803
18	Louisiana	April 30, 1812
19	Indiana	December 11, 1816
20	Mississippi	December 10, 1817
21	Illinois	December 3, 1818
22	Alabama	December 14, 1819
23	Maine	March 15, 1820
24	Missouri	August 10, 1821

Wars of the Era

FIRST BARBARY WAR, 1801-1805: Fought between the United States, Tripoli and Algiers. Barbary pirates attacked U.S. merchant ships, demanding a ransom for the sailors as well as a tribute from the United States.

BATTLE OF TIPPECANOE, 1811: The Prophet, a brother of the Shawnee chief Tecumseh, attacked settlers in Indiana Territory. William Henry Harrison led the force against the Shawnee.

CREEK WAR, 1814: Fought throughout Georgia and Alabama. Andrew Jackson led the fight against the Creek, who had attacked Fort Mims and massacred the settlers.

WAR OF 1812, 1812-1815: The United States declared war on the British in response to British impressments of U.S. sailors, British support of Indians attacking along the frontier and America's desire for Canada.

FIRST SEMINOLE WAR, 1817-1818: Fought in Florida between the Seminole (who defended runaway slaves) and forces led by Andrew Jackson. Spain was forced to relinquish its territory in Florida.

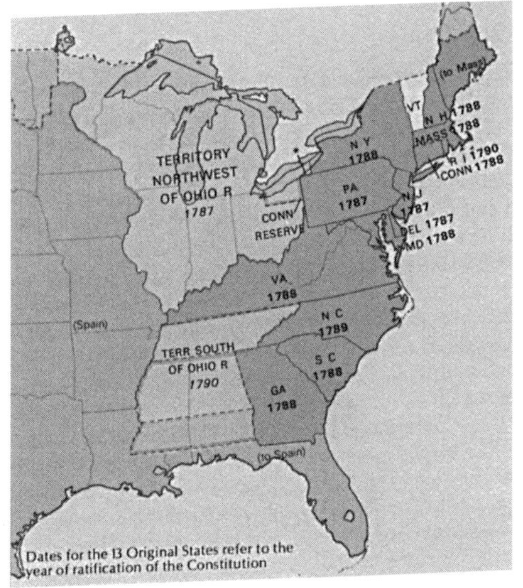

Territorial Growth, 1790
Courtesy of the University of Texas Libraries, The University of Texas at Austin

Causes of Death in the War of 1812

Infectious disease was the number one killer of soldiers fighting in the War of 1812, including:

- dysentery
- typhoid or "lake" fever
- pneumonia
- malaria
- measles
- smallpox

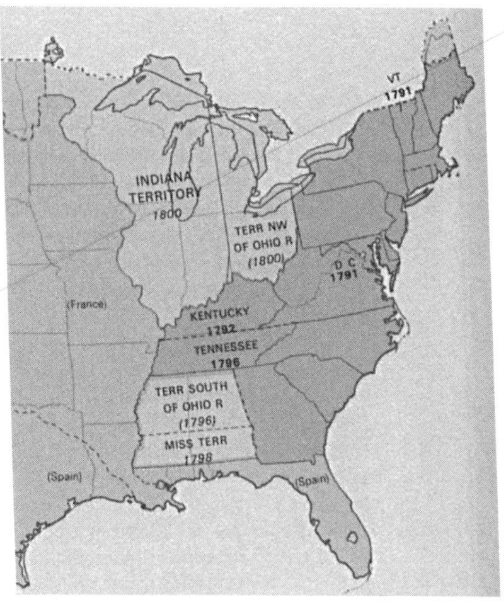

Territorial Growth, 1800
Courtesy of the University of Texas Libraries, The University of Texas at Austin

Of the estimated 20,000 soldiers, militiamen and Native warriors who died in the war, nearly three-quarters succumbed to something other than a battle wound.

Louisiana Purchase of 1803

Napoleon sold the Louisiana Territory (828,000 square miles) to the United States for less than 3-cents per acre. The sale doubled the size of the United States and encompassed all or part of 15 current U.S. states and two Canadian provinces:

- Arkansas
- Missouri
- Iowa
- Oklahoma
- Kansas
- Nebraska
- Minnesota
- North Dakota
- South Dakota
- New Mexico
- Texas
- Montana
- Wyoming
- Colorado
- Louisiana*
- Alberta
- Saskatchewan

**The area east of the Mississippi River and north of Lake Pontchartrain and the southwestern boundary of Louisiana were disputed with Spain until 1812.*

Lewis and Clark Explore New Territory

When America acquired the 828,000 square miles of the Louisiana Purchase, President Thomas Jefferson sent his secretary, Meriwether Lewis on an expedition to explore the new land.

Lewis and his co-captain, William Clark, led the Corps of Discovery to the Pacific Ocean and back to St. Louis, a journey that took from May 14, 1804 to September 23, 1806.

Quick Facts:

- The expedition took 863 days and traveled 7,689 miles.
- Only one man died during the expedition, Sgt. Charles Floyd.
- The Corps discovered 122 new animals and 178 new plants.
- William Clark's slave, York, was a member of the expedition; he was freed in 1811.
- Total cost was approximately $38,700.
- Lewis was shot in buttocks by Pierre Cruzatte, who mistook him for an elk.
- Lewis brought along Seaman, his Newfoundland retriever.

Direct Purchase of Federal Land

Settlers who wished to purchase land from the government could do so at a set price per acre and a minimum number of acres. Prices varied over time:

YEAR	PRICE PER ACRE	MINIMUM NUMBER OF ACRES
1787	$1.00	640
1796	$2.00	640
1800	$2.00	320
1804	$2.00	160
1820	$1.25	80

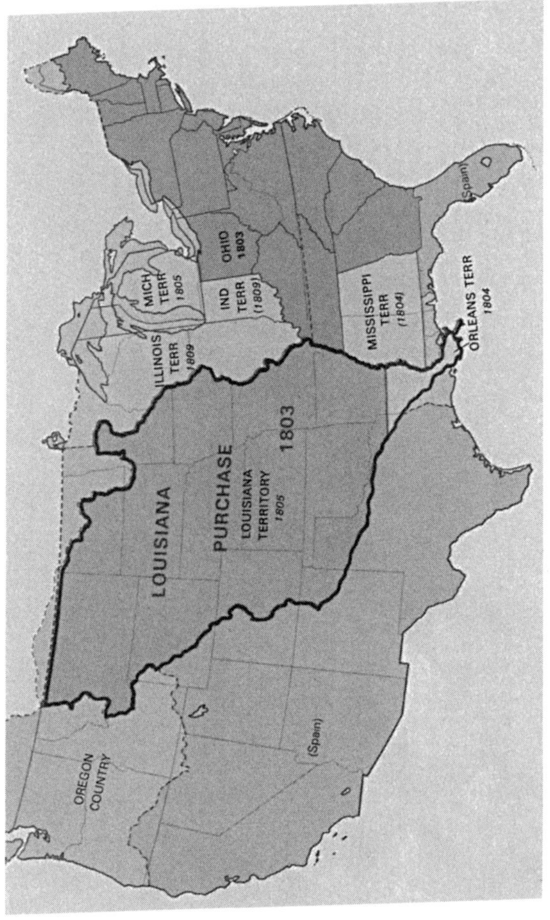

The Louisiana Purchase
Courtesy of the University of Texas Libraries, The University of Texas at Austin

Northwest Ordinance

Among its clauses was the ceding of all unsettled lands to the federal government, thus creating the public domain. This ordinance established a rectangular survey system designed to facilitate the transfer of federal lands to private citizens.

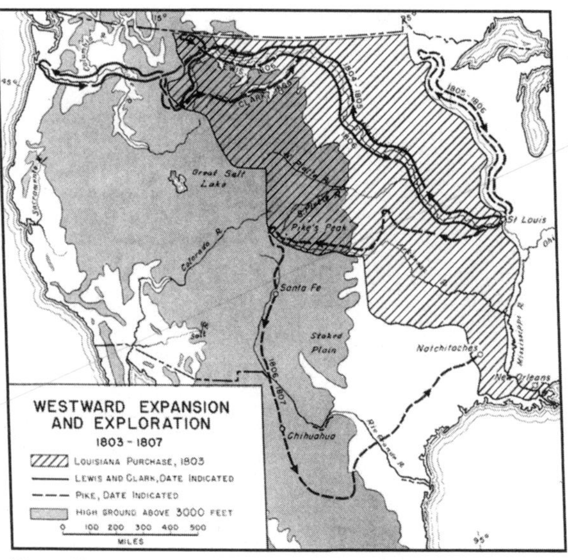

Westward Expansion and Exploration 1803-1807
Courtesy of the University of Texas Libraries, The University of Texas at Austin

Division of Land

For most of the United States west of the "Colonies," a system of rectangles was established to locate and specify the boundaries for land parcels. The system is known as the Rectangular Survey System. This provides for a unit of land approximately 24 miles square, bounded by base lines running east and west, and meridians running north and south. This 24-mile square is divided into areas six-miles square called townships. Townships contain 36 sections. Each section is approximately one-mile square and contains 640 acres.

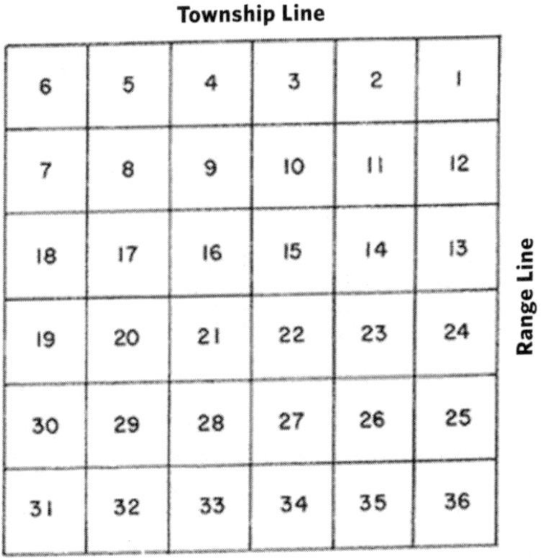

Township Line

6	5	4	3	2	1
7	8	9	10	11	12
18	17	16	15	14	13
19	20	21	22	23	24
30	29	28	27	26	25
31	32	33	34	35	36

Range Line

Missouri Compromise

Slavery was forbidden north of the Missouri Compromise line with the exception of the state of Missouri. To maintain an equal number of free and slaves states in the U.S. Senate, the compromise provided for the admission of Maine and Missouri. By 1821, the division of free and slaves states was:

FREE STATES	SLAVE STATES
Maine	Missouri
Vermont	Maryland
New Hampshire	Delaware
Massachusetts	Virginia
Illinois	Kentucky
Indiana	North Carolina
Ohio	South Carolina
Pennsylvania	Georgia
New York	Alabama
Connecticut	Mississippi
Rhode Island	Louisiana
New Jersey	Tennessee

1783–1830

Oregon Territory

James Cook explored the Oregon Coast in 1778 in search of the Northwest Passage. Soon thereafter, ships from several countries explored the region, with the goal of entering the lucrative fur trade. Robert Gray explored the Columbia River in 1792 while George Vancouver claimed Puget Sound for Great Britain. Lewis and Clark spent the winter of 1805 at Fort Clatsop, near the mouth of the Columbia. Following the Anglo-American Treaty of 1818, the region was jointly occupied by the United States and

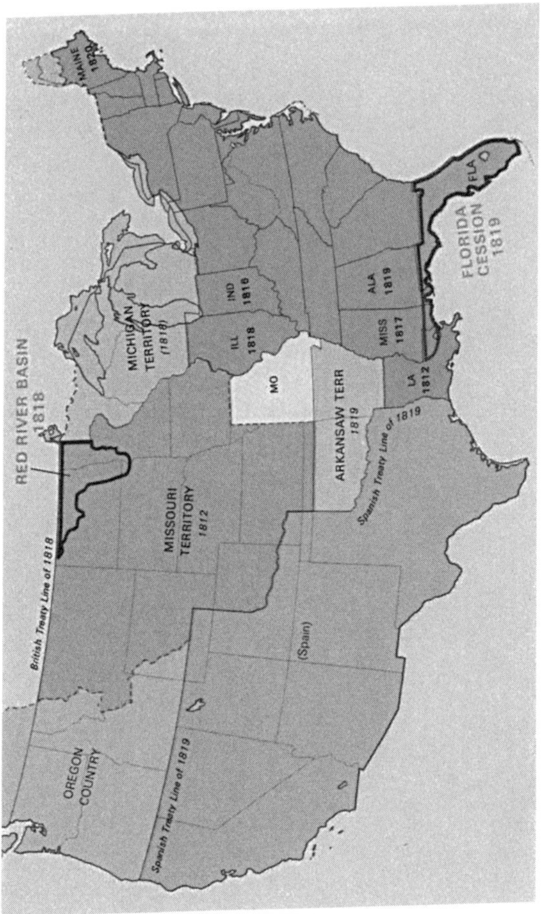

Territorial Growth 1820
Courtesy of the University of Texas Libraries, The University of Texas at Austin

1783–1830

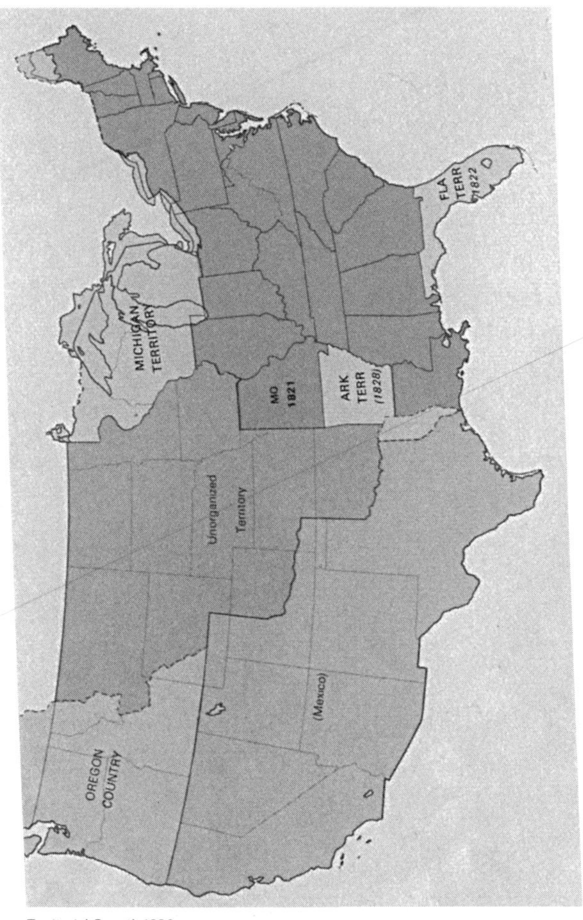

Territorial Growth 1830
Courtesy of the University of Texas Libraries, The University of Texas at Austin

Britain. Fort Astoria was the first permanent white settlement in the area. In a few decades the Oregon Trail would become the most highly traveled trail westward.

★ **TRIVIA** ★ On June 23, 1810, John Jacob Astor founds the Pacific Fur Company. The success of this trading company would make him the United States' first multi-millionaire and even when adjusted for inflation, one of the richest men in American history.

Along the Trail

Two famous western trails were heavily traveled during this era:

THE SANTA FE TRAIL: The major commerce route that connected Missouri with Santa Fe, New Mexico. Pioneered in 1821 by William Becknell, it was the main highway to New Mexico until 1880, and the route taken by the American Army during the Mexican-American War.

EL CAMINO REAL: Founded in 1769, it connected the 21 California missions, each built a day's travel apart. El Camino Real ran from San Diego to Sonoma.

Famous People of the Era

GEORGE WASHINGTON (1732-1799): First U.S. president, elected unanimously by the Electoral College in 1789; took the oath of office at Federal Hall in New York City; buried at Mount Vernon.

JOHN ADAMS (1735-1826): First vice-president and second president; first president to live in the White House; known for ending conflict with France through diplomacy and for signing the Alien and Sedition Acts of 1798; believed in following Washington's policy of staying out of European conflicts.

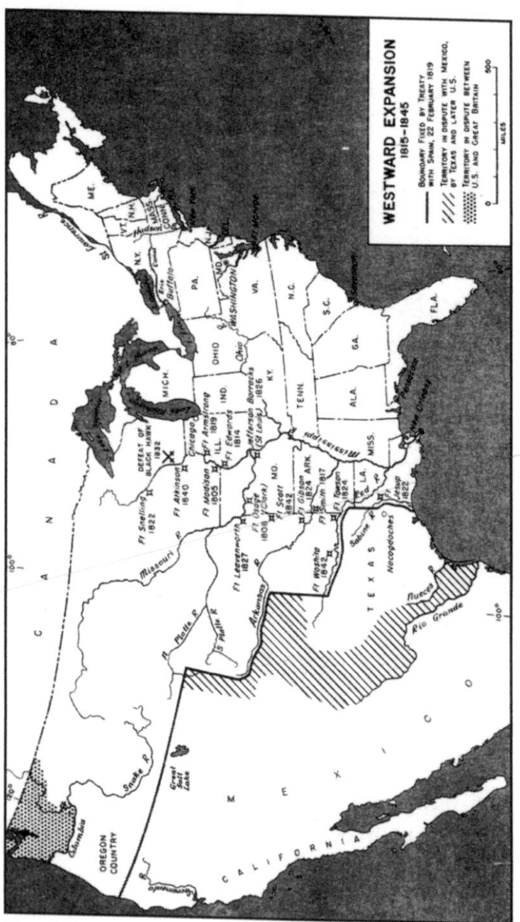

Westward Expansion and Exploration 1815–1845
Courtesy of the University of Texas Libraries, The University of Texas at Austin

THOMAS JEFFERSON (1743-1826): Secretary of state under Washington, vice-president under Adams and third U.S. president; purchased the Louisiana Territory from France and assigned his secretary, Meriwether Lewis, to lead the expedition to explore the new territory.

ALEXANDER HAMILTON (1755-1804): Served as Washington's aide during the Revolutionary War; became the first secretary of the treasury; helped found the U.S. Mint and the first national bank; his programs brought order to the chaotic financial system of the Confederation era.

JOHN JAY (1745-1829): Statesman, diplomat and first chief justice of the Supreme Court; supported a strong, centralized government; co-author of the "Federalist Papers," with Alexander Hamilton and James Madison.

DAVY CROCKETT (1786-1836): Frontiersman from Tennessee who became an American folk hero know as "King of the Wild Frontier;" was killed in the Battle of the Alamo during the Texas Revolution.

WILLIAM HENRY HARRISON (1773-1841): Aide-de-camp to Gen. "Mad Anthony" Wayne during the Revolutionary War; In 1798, he became secretary of the Northwest Territory and helped open the Indian land to settlement; In 1811 he led the attack on Tecumseh and The Prophet (Tecumseh's brother), at the Battle of Tippecanoe; commanded the Army of the Northwest in the War of 1812.

ANDREW JACKSON (1767-1845): Famous general who defeated the Creek Indians at the Battle of Horseshoe Bend (1814), and the British at the Battle of New Orleans (1815); Known as "Old Hickory" because of his aggressive and tough personality; favored a small central government; under his presidency, many criticized his strict enforcement of the Indian Removal Act, which forced Native Americans out of the Southeast and into what is now Oklahoma.

JOHN QUINCY ADAMS (1767-1848): Minister to Russia under Madison, secretary of state under Monroe; won the presidency over Andrew Jackson, who charged that a "corrupt bargain" had taken place and immediately began his campaign to become president in 1828. After Adams' 1828 defeat, he spent the rest of his life serving in the House of Representatives, until his death in 1848.

JAMES MADISON (1751-1836): Secretary of state under Jefferson; elected president in 1808; asked Congress to declare war against Britain on June 1, 1812, in response to British impressments of American seamen.

JAMES MONROE (1758-1831): Minister to France during Jefferson's presidency and helped negotiate the Louisiana Purchase; elected fifth president of the United States; best known for the Monroe Doctrine, which kept European nations out of the Americas and Russia from moving southward down the Pacific coast.

STEPHEN DECATUR (1779-1820): Played a major role in the development of the Navy and became the youngest man to reach the rank of captain; active in the Barbary Wars, but best known for his actions during the War of 1812, for which he was awarded the Congressional Gold Medal.

The Country's Presidents 1783–1830

PRESIDENT	LIFETIME	TIME IN OFFICE
George Washington	1732-1799	1789-1797
John Adams	1735-1826	1797-1801
Thomas Jefferson	1743-1826	1801-1809
James Madison	1751-1836	1809-1817
James Monroe	1758-1831	1817-1825
John Quincy Adams	1767-1848	1825-1829
Andrew Jackson	1767-1845	1829-1837

The Country's First Ladies 1783–1830

FIRST LADY	LIFETIME
Martha Dandridge Custis Washington	1731-1802
Abigail Smith Adams	1744-1818
Martha Wayles Skelton Jefferson	1748-1782
Dolley Payne Todd Madison	1768-1849
Elizabeth Kortright Monroe	1768-1830
Louisa Catherine Johnson Adams*	1775-1852
Rachel Donelson Jackson	1767-1828

**The only First Lady born outside the United States. Born in London where her father served as U.S. consul.*

The Age of Jackson

Andrew Jackson was the first presidential candidate to actively seek the support of the people, and it worked. In his 1828 election, twice as many voters cast ballots as they had in 1824, and four times as many as in 1820. Votes were divided among sectional lines, with Jackson winning the south and west while John Quincy Adams won the North (except Pennsylvania and

New York). Jackson was seen as the candidate of the common man in contrast with the wealthy supporters of Adams. Jackson's Democratic Republicans wanted a simple and less intrusive government. They opposed government spending and government favoritism. Andrew Jackson's presidency is known as the Era of Jacksonian Democracy.

The Death of George Washington

When Washington died on December 14, 1799, of epiglottis, the country went into mourning and mock funerals were held throughout the country. On December 26, 1799, in Philadelphia, 16 cannons were fired at daybreak, signaling the beginning of the mock funeral, with volleys repeated every half-hour throughout the morning. Next came a somber march with a riderless horse escorted by two marines. The horse carried an empty saddle, holsters, pistols and boots reversed in the stirrups, and was "trimmed with black—the head festooned with elegant black and white feathers—the American Eagle displayed in a rose upon the breast, and in a feather upon the head." In the midst of the procession, pallbearers carried an empty casket. The service was held at the German Lutheran Church with Richard Henry Lee reading the eulogy. Washington's death reached beyond American borders, with Napoleon ordering 10 days of mourning throughout France.

Inventions and Discoveries of the Era

INVENTION OR DISCOVERY	INVENTOR
Muskets with interchangeable parts	Eli Whitney
Binary stars	William Herschel
Steamboat	Robert Fulton
Miner's safety lamp (Dary lamp)	Sir Humphry Davy
Kaleidoscope	Sir David Brewster
Stethoscope	René Laennec

Epidemics

DISEASE	YEAR
Influenza	1793
Typhus	1793
Yellow Fever*	1793
Yellow Fever	1803
Smallpox	1830
Cholera	1830

* *The yellow fever epidemic of 1793 killed more than 4,000 people.*

Women and Medicine

From *A Compendium of the Theory and Practice of Midwifery* by Samuel Bard, published in 1812:

"In women of weak and delicate habits, bleeding is to be used with caution; and if too much blood be drawn, or it be imprudently repeated, much harm may be done, and a miscarriage will probably be the consequence."

Popular Foods of the Era

- Mutton Broth
- Partridge Soup
- Beefsteak Pie
- Brown Bread Pudding
- Baked Apples
- Orange Tart
- Venison Pastry
- Almond Custard
- Flummery
- Rice and Wheat Bread

★ **TRIVIA** ★ Tomatoes, a member of the nightshade family, were thought to be poisonous until Colonel Robert Gibbon Johnson ate one in public on September 28, 1820.

Recipes From the Era

Recipes from *New System of Domestic Cookery* by A Lady, 1807

A Charlotte

Cut as many very thin slices of white bread as will cover the bottom and line the sides of a baking dish, but first rub it thick with butter. Put apples, in thin slices, into the dish, in layers, till full, strewing sugar between, and bits of butter. In the meantime, soak as many thin slices of bread as will cover the whole, in warm milk, over which lay a plate, and a weight to keep the bread close on the apples. Bake slowly three hours. To a middling-sized dish use half a pound of butter in the whole.

Eel Broth

Clean half a pound of small eels, and set them on with three pints of water, some parsley, one slice of onion, a few pepper-corns; let them simmer till the eels are broken, and the broth good. Add salt, and strain it off. The above should make three half-pints of broth.

Songs of the Era

- "Decatur and the Navy"
- "The Eighth of January"
- "The Lakes of Pontchartrain"
- "Perry's Victory"
- "The Ship Boys"
- "Silent Night! Holy Night!"
- "The Star-Spangled Banner"
- "The Warrior's Return"

"The Battle of Baltimore"

(lyrics & music by Martin O'Malley)

There's an awful fright on the streets tonight
far below the harvest moon.
Washington lies sacked and burned.
Their guns will be here soon.

But, as I ride forth to Armistead's fort
know that my thoughts will be of you.
Not an inch we'll yield
beneath God's shield
with our neighbors strong and true.

(Chorus) We'll stand alone for love and liberty.
We'll stand alone for this one land of the free.
And when the bombs of Hell come raining down tonight,
we'll stand alone for Baltimore and liberty
we'll stand alone for Baltimore and liberty.

Not long ago it seemed as though our future was so bright
Peace it smiled on every mile beneath the stars and stripes.
But now the chains of tyranny are grinding at our door
And America's young fate now rests in the hands of Baltimore.

So now my love the eagle's nest is ours to win or lose.
Pray tonight dawn's early light will bring you victory's news.
And when our foe has turned to run, and his heel has left
our shore
Our countrymen will sing their praise of the town of Baltimore.

★ **TRIVIA** ★ The valiant defense of Baltimore's Fort McHenry inspired Francis Scott Key to write "The Star-Spangled Banner." To this day, the American flag flies over Fort McHenry 24 hours a day by special order of the White House. When a star is added or if there is a new design for the flag, Fort McHenry is the first location to fly the new flag.

Books and Poems of the Era

- *History of New York* by Washington Irving, 1809
- *The Lady of the Lake* by Walter Scott, 1810
- *Sense and Sensibility* by Jane Austen, 1811
- *Kubla Khan* by Samuel Taylor Coleridge, 1816
- *Rip van Winkle* by Washington Irving, 1819
- *Frankenstein* by Mary Wollstonecraft Shelley, 1823
- *Last of the Mohicans* by James Fenimore Cooper, 1826
- *The Birds of America* by John James Audubon, 1827

Most Popular Names 1800–1810

MALE	FEMALE
John	Mary
William	Elizabeth
James	Sarah
Thomas	Nancy
George	Ann
Joseph	Catherine
Samuel	Margaret
Henry	Jane
David	Susan
Daniel	Hannah

The First Federal Census

The first U.S. federal census was taken in 1790 and every 10 years thereafter. In 1790, the population was:

STATE	POPULATION
Connecticut	237,655
Delaware	59,094
Georgia	82,548
Kentucky (territory)	73,677
Maine (territory)	90,540
Maryland	319,728
Massachusetts	378,787
New Hampshire	141,895
New Jersey	184,139
New York	340,120
North Carolina	393,751
Pennsylvania	434,373
Rhode Island	68,825
South Carolina	249,073
Vermont (territory)	85,539
Virginia	747,610

Total Population of the United States, 1830

By the time of the fifth federal census (1830), the total population was 12,858,670.

STATE	POPULATION
Alabama	309,527
Arkansas Territory	30,388
Connecticut	297,675
Delaware	76,748

STATE	POPULATION
District of Columbia	39,834
Florida Territory	34,730
Georgia	516,823
Illinois	157,445
Indiana	343,031
Kentucky	687,917
Louisiana	215,730
Maine	399,437
Maryland	447,040
Massachusetts	610,408
Michigan Territory	31,639
Mississippi	136,621
Missouri	140,455
New Hampshire	269,328
New Jersey	320,823
New York	1,918,608
North Carolina	737,987
Ohio	935,884
Pennsylvania	1,348,233
Rhode Island	97,199
Tennessee	681,903
South Carolina	581,185
Vermont	280,657
Virginia	1,211,405

Top 10 U.S. Cities by Population in 1790

New York City	33,131
Philadelphia	28,522
Boston	18,320
Charlestown, South Carolina	16,359
Baltimore	13,503
Northern Liberties, Pennsylvania (Annexed by Philadelphia in 1854)	9,913
Salem, Massachusetts	7,921
Newport, Rhode Island	6,716
Providence, Rhode Island	6,380
Marblehead, Massachusetts	5,661

Top 10 U.S. Cities by Population in 1830

New York City	202,589
Baltimore	80,620
Philadelphia	80,462
Boston	61,392
New Orleans	46,082
Charleston, South Carolina	30,289
Northern Liberties, Pennsylvania (Annexed by Philadelphia in 1854)	28,872
Cincinnati, Ohio	24,831
Albany, New York	24,209
Southwark District, Pennsylvania	20,581

Top 10 Immigration by Country

COUNTRY	NUMBER OF EMIGRANTS IN 1820	NUMBER OF EMIGRANTS 1821-1830
Ireland	3,614	50,724
England	1,782	14,055
Germany	968	6,761
France	371	8,497
Scotland	268	2,912
Canada/Newfoundland	209	2,277
West Indies	164	3,834
Spain	139	2,477
Netherlands	49	1,078
Switzerland	31	3,226

Major Immigration Ports of Entry

- Mobile, Alabama
- Wilmington, Delaware
- Savannah, Georgia
- Baltimore
- Boston
- New York City
- Philadelphia
- Charleston, South Carolina
- New Orleans
- Portland-Falmouth, Maine

Official Census Dates of the Era

1790: August 2
1800: August 4
1810: August 6
1820: August 7
1830: June 1

Non-Population Censuses of the Era

MANUFACTURING AND INDUSTRY SCHEDULES: 1810, 1820

Colonial, Territorial and State Censuses of the Era

ALABAMA: 1706-1819 (various years); 1820 (eight counties)

ARIZONA: 1801

ARKANSAS: 1823, 1829 (fragments)

CALIFORNIA: 1793, 1796, 1797, 1798 (various areas)

FLORIDA: 1783; 1784-1786; 1790; 1793; 1813; 1814; 1815; 1820 (Pensacola and Escambia River Areas); 1824 (fragments); 1825 (Leon County)

GEORGIA: 1787-1866 (various years; fragments survive)

ILLINOIS: 1810 (Randolph County, as Indiana Territory); 1818; 1820-1845 (every five years, various counties)

INDIANA: 1807; 1816 (postmasters); 1820-on (various years, males older than 21)

LOUISIANA: 1784-1786, 1788-1790, 1795, 1798, 1799, 1803, 1805 (various communities); 1792-1806, 1809 (Nacogdoches); 1791 (New Orleans); 1812-1815 (War of 1812 pensioners)

MICHIGAN: 1710, various through 1792 (Detroit area); 1796 (Wayne County); 1827

MISSISSIPPI: 1784; 1787; 1788; 1790 (Tobacco growers in the Spanish Natchez district); 1792 (Natchez); 1794; 1798-1817 (various years) 1805, 1810, 1813, 1815-1818, 1820, 1830

MISSOURI: 1770-1804 (various areas); 1797, 1803 (New Madrid); 1817, 1819 (St. Charles)

NEW JERSEY: 1824-1832 (Paterson)

NEW MEXICO: 1750-1845 (various years and areas); 1788 and 1790 (El Paso del Norte)

NEW YORK: 1825

NORTH CAROLINA: 1784-1787; 1793-1840 (Black craftsmen)

SOUTH CAROLINA: 1829 (Fairfield and Laurens districts)

TENNESSEE: 1770-1790 (Cumberland settlements)

TEXAS: 1783-1836 (various years and areas), 1828

VERMONT: 1785

VIRGINIA: 1782-1786

4

Growth, War and Reconstruction

1830 to **1870**

About the Era

America was growing. From 1832 to 1867, 13 new states joined the Union and countless thousands traveled to western territories along the Oregon Trail. In addition, the country added 586,412 additional square miles with the acquisition of Alaska. With growth came dissension, which of the new territories would allow slavery and which would remain free?

This question was at the heart of legislation designed to head off armed conflict, including the Missouri Compromise of 1820, the Compromise of 1850 and the Kansas-Nebraska Act. Although each provided a short period of relief, the 1860 election of Abraham Lincoln brought a war that would divide the country along sectional and philosophical lines. In America's first 100 years of existence, over 683,000 Americans lost their lives in wars; the Civil War accounted for 623,026 of that total.

Events That Shaped the Era

1836 Defeat of Texas loyalists at the Alamo

Texas Declaration of Independence

1837 Financial panic

1838 Trail of Tears (Forced relocation of Native Americans following the Indian Removal Act of 1830; 4,000 died en route)

1841 United States v. *The Amistad* court case reaches U.S. Supreme Court

1845 Annexation of Texas

1845 Thoreau withdraws to Walden Pond

1845 Rain in Ireland exacerbates the Great Potato Famine and encourages emigration

1846 Donner Party tragedy

1847 Refugees from Irish potato famine begin arriving in large numbers

1848 California Gold Rush

Seneca Falls Convention (Women's rights convention)

1850 Compromise of 1850 (Delayed the Civil War by a decade)

Slave trade abolished in Washington, D.C.

1852 Publication of Harriet Beecher Stowe's *Uncle Tom's Cabin*

1853 First major U.S. rail disaster kills 48 at Norwalk, Conn.

1853 Gadsden Purchase (Purchase of southern Arizona and southwestern New Mexico)

1854 Kansas-Nebraska Act (Created Kansas and Nebraska and allowed citizens to decide whether or not to allow slavery)

1857 Financial panic

Dred Scott Decision (Supreme Court ruled that people brought to America as slaves were not citizens and were not protected under the Constitution)

1858 Lincoln's "house divided" speech

1859 John Brown's raid on Harper's Ferry

1860 Lincoln elected president

South Carolina's secession

1861 Attack on Fort Sumter

1862 Homestead Act (opened the west to settlement)

1863 Emancipation Proclamation (Freed slaves in the rebellious states)

First all-black regiment authorized

Battle of Gettysburg (Largest number of casualties in the Civil War)

1865 Lincoln assassinated

Thirteenth Amendment ratified (Outlawed slavery)

1867 Purchase of Alaska from Russia, adding 586,412 square miles to the United States

Reconstruction Acts of 1867 (Detailed the steps necessary for a Confederate state to be readmitted to the Union)

1868 Ulysses S. Grant elected president

1868-1869 Great Lakes storms sink or run aground more than 3,000 ships, killing 500-plus people

1869 The transcontinental railroad was linked at Promontory Summit, Utah

1869 110 die in a coal mine disaster in Avondale, Pennsylvania.

The Order of Statehood 1836–1867

NUMBER BY ADMISSION	STATE	ADMITTED	ORIGIN
25	Arkansas	June 15, 1836	Arkansas Territory
26	Michigan	January 26, 1837	Michigan Territory
27	Florida	March 3, 1845	Florida Territory
28	Texas	December 29, 1845	Republic of Texas
29	Iowa	December 28, 1846	Iowa Territory
30	Wisconsin	May 29, 1848	Wisconsin Territory
31	California	September 9, 1850	Mexican Cession
32	Minnesota	May 11, 1858	Minnesota Territory
33	Oregon	February 14, 1859	Oregon Territory
34	Kansas	January 29, 1861	Kansas Territory
35	West Virginia	June 20, 1863	Virginia
36	Nevada	October 31, 1864	Nevada Territory
37	Nebraska	March 1, 1867	Nebraska Territory

The Nat Turner Rebellion

In 1831, Nat Turner, a Virginia slave staged a bloody revolt, killing almost 60 slave owners and their families. Turner had hoped to raise a slave rebellion; however, a white militia was formed that dispersed Turner's followers. In retaliation, whites killed slaves at random, with 48 slaves receiving formal trials and 20 hanged, among them Nat Turner.

Manifest Destiny

Manifest Destiny is a term coined in 1845 by John L. O'Sullivan, editor of the *Democratic Review*. He wrote "our manifest destiny is to overspread the continent allotted by Providence for the free

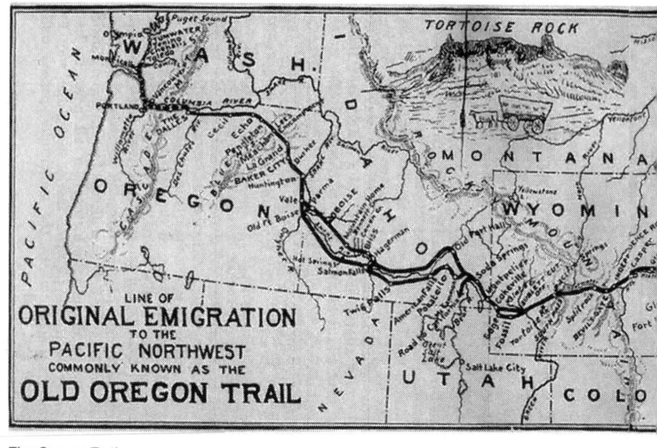

The Oregon Trail
Courtesy of the University of Texas Libraries, The University of Texas at Austin

development of our yearly multiplying millions." For O'Sullivan, the term meant that the United States had a divinely inspired mission to settle the entire continent. To Southerners, this philosophy meant the ability to export slavery into new territories; for Northerners the chance to expand business and industry far west.

Along the Oregon Trail

Although both the United States and Britain could settle in Oregon Territory, based on an 1818 agreement, by 1842 a large number of American settlers began traveling the Oregon Trail, lured by reports of a mild climate and fertile soil in the Willamette Valley. By the Civil War, more than 350,000 people traveled the trail, either to Oregon or California. Of those, some 34,000 died along the way, about 17 deaths per mile. The migrant wagons carved 5-foot-deep ruts in the sandstone, which are still visible in Southern Wyoming.

Food on the Oregon Trail

From *The Emigrant's Guide to Oregon and California*, by Lansford W. Hastings, 1845:

"In procuring supplies for this journey, the emigrant should provide himself with, at least

- 200 pounds of flour or meal
- 150 pounds of bacon
- 10 pounds of coffee
- 20 pounds of sugar
- 10 pounds of salt

Very few cooking utensils should be taken, as they very, much increase the load, to avoid which, is always a consideration of paramount importance. A baking-kettle, frying-pan, tea-kettle, tea-pot, and coffee-pot are all the furniture of this kind, that is essential, which, together with tin plates, tin cups, ordinary knives, forks, spoons, and a coffee-mill, should constitute the entire kitchen apparatus."

The California Gold Rush by the Numbers

When James Marshall discovered gold at Sutter's Mill, the face of California was changed forever.

TIMEFRAME	POPULATION
Pre-gold rush	14,000
1850	93,000
1852	250,000
1860	380,000

- 77 percent of the 1850 population were male, aged 15–40.
- More than 1 percent of the entire nation had moved to California in just four years.
- In 1850, there were 624 miners for every 1,000 people in the state.
- A slice of bread during the gold rush sold for one dollar; two dollars if buttered.
- From 1792 to 1847 the cumulative U.S. gold production was 37 tons; California's production in 1849 alone exceeded this figure. Annual production from 1848 to 1857 averaged 76 tons.
- Immigrants came to California from the Far East, Mexico, South America and the East Coast.
- The trip from the East Coast to California took about six months (from April to September) and cost approximately $200.

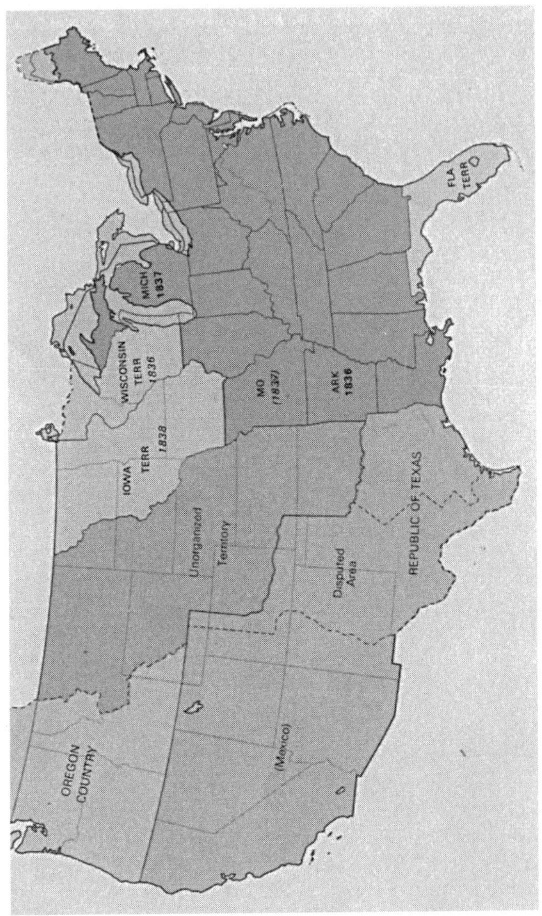

Territorial Growth, 1840
Courtesy of the University of Texas Libraries, The University of Texas at Austin

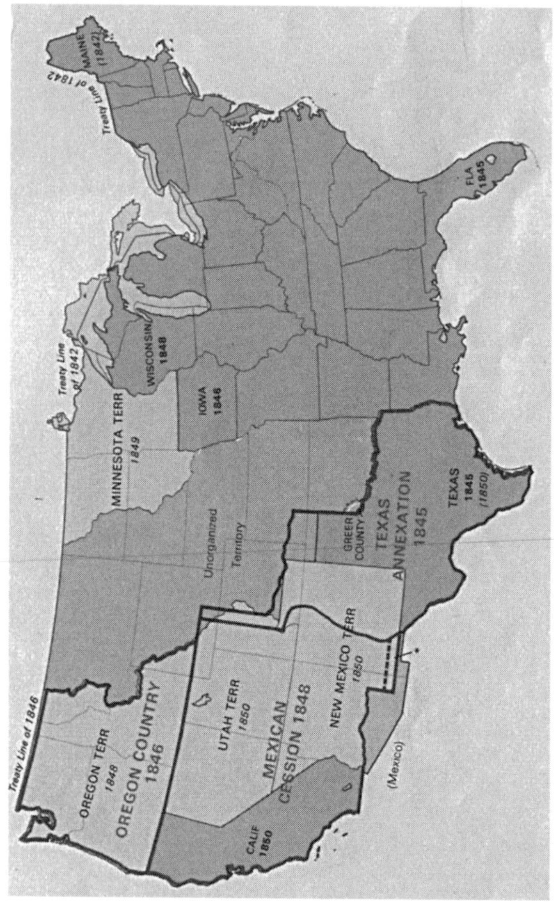

Territorial Growth, 1850
Courtesy of the University of Texas Libraries, The University of Texas at Austin

The Railroad

In the decade prior to the Civil War, the United States saw a boom in transportation via the railroad. An extensive rail system was laid in the North with a much simpler one in the South. Unfortunately, railroad companies built lines using different track gauges, hindering an efficient flow of goods. However, the transportation revolution decreased travel times immensely. In 1800, it required one day to travel from New York City to Philadelphia (a distance of about 100 miles). In 1860, the railroad could take a traveler from New York all the way to Cleveland, Ohio (a distance of about 500 miles) in a single day.

Bleeding Kansas

From 1854 to 1861, the Kansas-Missouri border was the scene of some of the most violent pro- and antislavery conflict in the country. This period was known as Bleeding Kansas. The Kansas-Nebraska Act of 1854, allowed citizens to decide whether Kansas would be a free or slave state; as a result proponents on both sides of the question poured into Kansas. Jayhawkers was the term given to militant "free-staters;" while pro-slavers were called Border Ruffians.

Violence escalated when proslavery men burned the Free State Hotel in Lawrence and ransacked homes and stores. John Brown, the abolitionist, retaliated by murdering five men. The last major outbreak of violence took place near Fort Scott, on the Kansas-Missouri border, called the *Marais des Cygnes* massacre. During the attack, Border Ruffians killed five Free State men.

The Pony Express

The Pony Express was a mail service that operated from April 3, 1860, to October 1861. Western-going riders started at St. Joseph, Missouri., while those heading east began at Sacramento, California. Riders followed a route that took them through what is now Kansas, Nebraska, Colorado, Wyoming, Utah and Nevada.

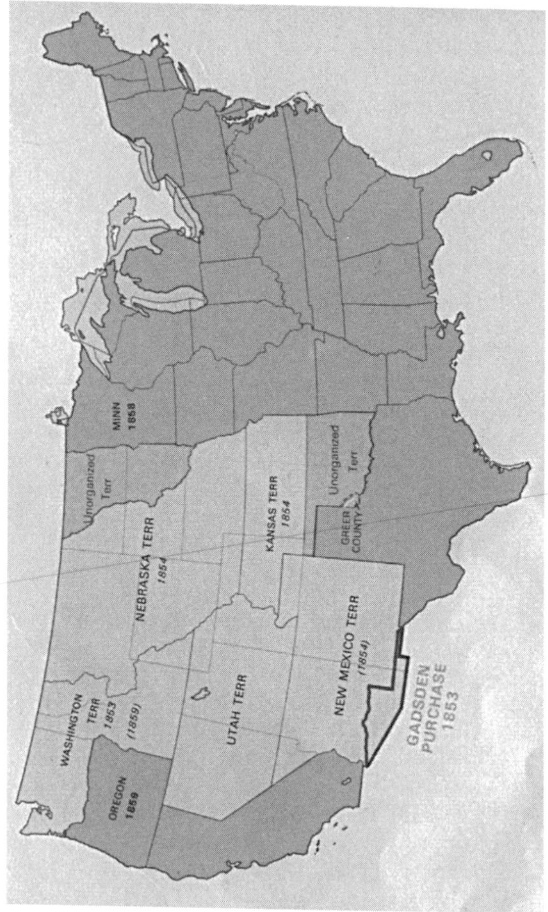

Territorial Growth, 1860
Courtesy of the University of Texas Libraries, The University of Texas at Austin

Numbered among its young riders were Buffalo Bill Cody, Robert Haslam, Jack Keetley, Billy Tate (aged 14, who was killed by Paiutes), Johnny Fry and Billy Richardson. During its early days, the Pony Express charged five dollars for a half-ounce letter.

Wars of the Era

BLACK HAWK WAR, 1832: Conflict between the Sauk American Indians, led by Black Hawk, and the United States; at the heart of the conflict was a disputed 1804 treaty that transferred Sauk land to the government. Black Hawk's incursions across the Mississippi River into Illinois were attempts to regain tribal lands. A 23-year-old Abraham Lincoln served in the volunteer militia during the war for three months in 1832.

MEXICAN-AMERICAN WAR, 1846-1848: Mexico lost nearly half of its territory, including the present American Southwest from Texas to California, to the United States. Then-Congressman Abraham Lincoln was a vocal opponent of the war. This war was the proving ground for future Civil War generals, including Ulysses S. Grant, Robert E. Lee, George Meade, James Longstreet and Thomas "Stonewall" Jackson.

CIVIL WAR, 1861-1865: Struggle between federalists who believed in a strong central government and anti-federalists who believed the states should have the right to determine their own laws. When Abraham Lincoln was elected, South Carolina seceded from the Union, followed by Mississippi, Florida, Alabama, Georgia, Louisiana, Texas, Virginia, Arkansas, Tennessee and North Carolina. The Confederate States of America was officially formed on February 9, 1861.

Events That Shaped the Civil War

OCTOBER 16, 1859: Abolitionist John Brown seizes federal arsenal at Harper's Ferry, subsequently captured and hanged.

NOVEMBER 6, 1860: Abraham Lincoln elected president.

DECEMBER 20, 1860: South Carolina votes to secede from the Union.

JANUARY–FEBRUARY 1861: Six more Southern states secede.

FEBRUARY 9, 1861: Jefferson Davis elected president of the Confederate States of America.

APRIL 12, 1861: Fort Sumter is fired upon by Southern troops; surrenders April 14.

APRIL 15, 1861: Lincoln calls for 75,000 men to volunteer for the Federal army.

APRIL–JUNE 1861: Four more states join the Confederacy.

JULY 21, 1861: First Battle of Bull Run (Manassas).

JULY 1861: Federal blockade of Southern ports.

MARCH 9, 1862: *CSS Virginia* sinks two Union warships off the coast of Virginia; engages in battle against *USS Monitor.*

APRIL 6–7, 1862: Battle of Shiloh (Tennessee).

APRIL 25, 1862: David Farragut captures New Orleans.

AUGUST 28–30, 1862: Second Battle of Bull Run; more than 22,000 casualties (killed, wounded, missing in action).

SEPTEMBER 17, 1862: Battle of Antietam (Maryland).

DECEMBER 11–15, 1862: Battle of Fredericksburg (Virginia); devastating loss for Union army.

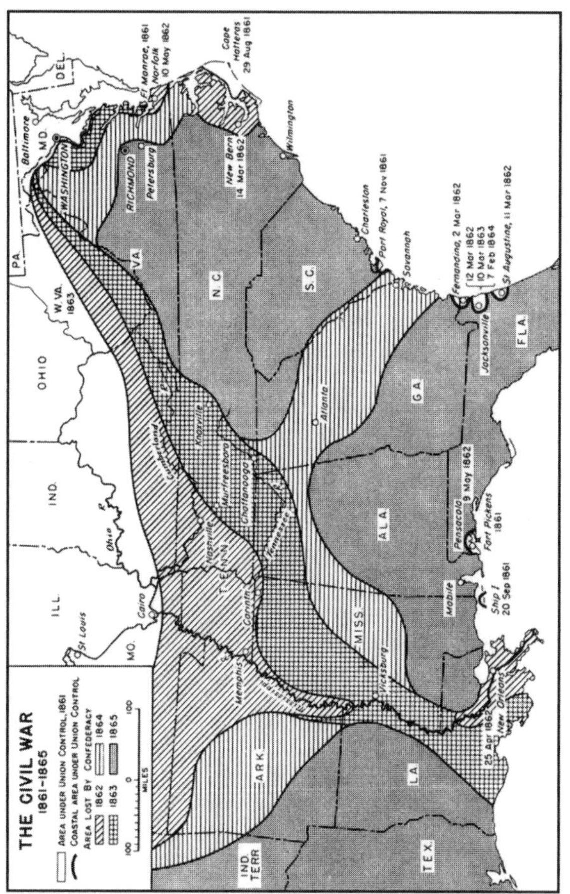

Territory lost by the Confederacy 1862-1865
Courtesy of the University of Texas Libraries, The University of Texas at Austin

JANUARY 1, 1863: Emancipation Proclamation issued.

APRIL 30–MAY 6, 1863: Battle of Chancellorsville (Virginia); crippling loss for the South with the death of Thomas "Stonewall" Jackson.

JULY 1–3, 1863: Battle of Gettysburg (Pennsylvania); Federal army fails to pursue Lee after his defeat here.

JULY 4, 1863: Siege of Vicksburg (Mississippi) ends with surrender to General Grant.

JULY 13–16, 1863: Irish workers initiate draft riots.

NOVEMBER 19, 1863: Lincoln dedicates the battlefield at Gettysburg, gives his famous Gettysburg Address.

FEBRUARY 17, 1864: Confederate submarine *CSS Hunley* lost in action.

FEBRUARY 25, 1864: First Union prisoners of war arrive at Andersonville Prison, Georgia.

MARCH 9, 1864: Ulysses S. Grant made commander-in-chief of entire Union army.

MAY 31–JUNE 12, 1864: Battle of Cold Harbor (Virginia); more than 7,000 men are killed in 20 minutes.

SEPTEMBER 2, 1864: Union troops occupy Atlanta.

NOVEMBER 8, 1864: Abraham Lincoln reelected president.

DECEMBER 21, 1864: General Sherman captures Savannah.

APRIL 2, 1865: General Lee evacuates Richmond.

APRIL 9, 1865: General Lee surrenders at Appomattox Courthouse (Virginia).

APRIL 14, 1865: John Wilkes Booth assassinates Abraham Lincoln.

MAY 10, 1865: Jefferson Davis is captured.

MAY 23-24, 1865: Grand Review; men from the Army of the Potomac and the Army of Georgia march through the streets of Washington, D.C.

The Election of 1860

CANDIDATE	PARTY	ELECTORAL VOTE	POPULAR VOTE
Abraham Lincoln	Republican	180	1,865,908
Stephen Douglas	N. Democrat	12	1,380,202
John C. Breckinridge	S. Democrat	72	848,019
John Bell	Constitutional Union	39	590,901

★ **TRIVIA** ★ Mary Todd Lincoln had ties to three of the four Presidential candidates; she was courted by Lincoln and Douglas and was a cousin of John C. Breckinridge.

---

10 Costliest Battles of the Civil War

BATTLE	PLACE	DATE	CASUALTIES
Gettysburg	Pennsylvania	July 1-3, 1863	51,112
Chickamauga	Georgia	September 19-20, 1863	34,624
Chancellorsville	Virginia	April 30-May 6, 1863	30,764

BATTLE	PLACE	DATE	CASUALTIES
Spotsylvania	Virginia	May 8-21, 1864	30,000
The Wilderness	Virginia	May 5-7, 1864	29,800
Shiloh	Tennessee	April 6-7, 1862	23,746
Stone's River	Tennessee	December 31, 1862-January 2, 1863	23,515
Antietam	Maryland	September 16-18, 1862	22,717
Second Manassas	Virginia	August 29-30, 1862	22,177
Fort Donelson	Tennessee	February 11-16, 1862	16,537

★ **TRIVIA** ★ On July 4, 1863, following a 47 day siege, the town of Vicksburg, Mississippi, surrendered to Union Troops. The residents of Vicksburg did not celebrate the national 4th of July again until 1945.

★ **TRIVIA** ★ General Phil Sheridan was a master of the "scorched earth policy"; destroying anything that could be salvageable to the enemy. In July of 1874, Sheridan's troops laid waste to the Shenandoah Valley in retribution for its people providing refuge for the Confederate cavalry. During the fall, Sheridan's troops destroyed grain supplies, barns, farming implements and gristmills.

Reconstruction

As the Civil War drew to a close, President Lincoln had already begun plans for reconstruction. Disposed to grant generous conditions to the South, Lincoln wanted to grant a pardon to all rebels who would lay down their arms and take a loyalty oath. His pardon included all but the topmost leaders.

Lincoln's "soft" reconstruction was opposed by Radical Republicans in Congress led by Thaddeus Stevens. While Lincoln

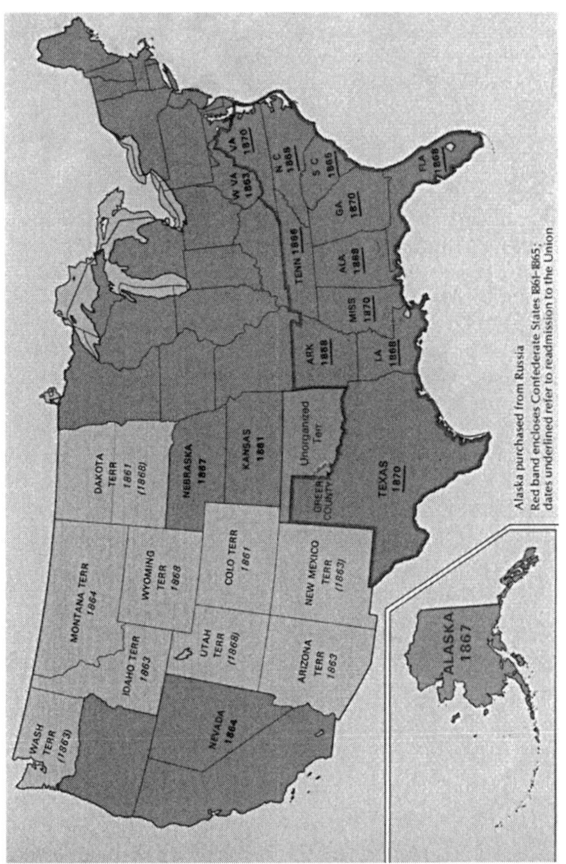

Territorial Growth, 1870
Courtesy of the University of Texas Libraries, The University of Texas at Austin

preached "malice toward none, with charity for all," Stevens believed Southerners should "eat the fruit of foul rebellion." Stevens wanted to confiscate plantations and divide their land among freed slaves. While President Andrew Johnson favored Lincoln's plans, Congress blocked a fair and just reconstruction.

For the white Southerner, the new way of life was intolerable. With Radical Republication rule and Carpetbagger corruption, a Southern aristocrat wrote to Thaddeus Stevens "We are the children of the Lees, Clays, Henrys and Jacksons . . . tell me if we are to be ruled by the dregs of society."

In retaliation for unfair taxes and the inability to have a voice in local politics, Southern whites turned their fury towards blacks and Carpetbaggers. The Mississippi state legislature passed a series of laws, which regulated the life and labor of blacks. Known as the "black codes," they legally established segregation and policies that all but returned blacks to slavery.

Famous People of the Era

COCHISE (c.1805-1874): Leader of an Apache uprising that began in 1861

GERONIMO (c.1829-1909): American Indian who fought against Mexico and the United States; became a celebrity later in life

SITTING BULL (c.1831-1890): Leader of the Hunkpapa band of the Sioux

CHIEF JOSEPH (1840-1904): Leader of the Wallowa band of Nez Perce; renowned as a peacemaker

CRAZY HORSE (c.1840-1877): War leader of the Oglala Lakota; his first major success was against troops from Fort Phil Kearny in 1866

CHRISTOPHER "KIT" CARSON (1809-1868): Indian fighter, trapper and guide

JAMES BUTLER "WILD BILL" HICKOK (1837-1876): Frontier gambler, scout and gunfighter

WILLIAM FREDERICK "BUFFALO BILL" CODY (1846-1917): Soldier, scout and buffalo hunter

JULES VERNE (1828-1905): French author, considered the Father of Science Fiction. Among his works are *Twenty Thousand Leagues Under the Sea* and *Journey to the Center of the Earth*

JESSE WOODSON JAMES (1847-1882): Notorious outlaw from Missouri

ELIZABETH CADY STANTON (1815-1902): Social activist and leader in the women's rights movement

SUSAN BROWNELL ANTHONY (1820-1906): Co-founder of the first Women's Temperance Movement

P.T. BARNUM (1810-1891): American showman, founder of the Ringling Bros. and Barnum & Bailey Circus

CLARA BARTON (1821-1912): Civil War nurse and founder of the American Red Cross

ZACHARY TAYLOR (1784-1850): Twelfth president of the United States; Veteran of the War of 1812, Black Hawk War and Mexican-American War

FRANCIS PARKMAN (1823-1893): American historian, best known for his *The Oregon Trail: Sketches of Prairie and Rocky-Mountain Life*

RALPH WALDO EMERSON (1803-1882): Philosopher and poet, leader of the Transcendentalist movement

HENRY DAVID THOREAU (1817-1862): Writer who influenced philosophers, political leaders and ordinary men and women in many parts of the world

NATHANIEL HAWTHORNE (1804-1864): American novelist, known for *The Scarlet Letter*

HERMAN MELVILLE (1819-1891): Wrote *Moby-Dick*, a novel about a whale hunt that has become an American classic

MARK TWAIN (SAMUEL LANGHORNE CLEMENS) (1835-1910): American newspaperman and novelist, best known for *The Adventures of Tom Sawyer*

EDGAR ALLAN POE (1809-1849): Poet and literary critic; considered the master of mystery fiction

WALT WHITMAN (1819-1892): Civil War nurse, poet, essayist; His *Leaves of Grass* was considered a controversial work during his lifetime

EMILY DICKINSON (1830-1886): Introverted and reclusive poet who lived a sheltered life in Amherst, Massachusetts; less than a dozen poems were published during her lifetime

ABRAHAM LINCOLN (1809-1865): Sixteenth president of the United States; led the United States through the Civil War; assassinated, in 1865; before being elected president in 1860 he had served in the Black Hawk War and worked as a lawyer on the frontier

MARY TODD LINCOLN (1818-1882): Wife of Abraham Lincoln, daughter of a wealthy Kentucky banker

JOHN WILKES BOOTH (1838-1865): American actor and Southern sympathizer; assassinated Abraham Lincoln on April 14, 1865; was shot and killed while hiding from an Army patrol

GORDON MEADE (1815-1872): Veteran of the Second Seminole and Mexican-American Wars; defeated by Robert E. Lee at the Battle of Gettysburg; President Lincoln replaced Meade as commanding general of the U.S. Army with Ulysses S. Grant.

ULYSSES S. GRANT (1822-1885): Eighteenth president of the United States; West Point graduate and veteran of the Mexican-American War; his leadership of the U.S. Army during the Civil War brought victory to Northern forces

JEFFERSON DAVIS (1808-1889): President of the Confederate States of America; graduate of West Point and a veteran of the Mexican-American War

ROBERT E. LEE (1807-1870): Commander of the Confederate Army of Northern Virginia; veteran of the Mexican-American War and Superintendent of the U.S. Military Academy

THOMAS "STONEWALL" JACKSON (1824-1863): Confederate general and strategist; wounded at the Battle of Chancellorsville by friendly fire and died a week later of complications

NATHAN BEDFORD FORREST (1821-1877): Confederate general; became the Grand Wizard of the Ku Klux Klan

The Country's Presidents 1830–1870

NUMBER BY DATE IN OFFICE	PRESIDENT	LIFETIME	YEARS IN OFFICE
7	Andrew Jackson	1767-1845	1829-1837
8	Martin Van Buren	1782-1862	1837-1841
9	William Henry Harrison	1773-1841	March 4, 1841-April 4, 1841
10	John Tyler	1790-1862	1841-1845
11	James K. Polk	1795-1849	1845-1849
12	Zachary Taylor	1784-1850	1849-1850
13	Millard Fillmore	1800-1874	1850-1853
14	Franklin Pierce	1804-1869	1853-1857
15	James Buchanan	1791-1868	1857-1861
16	Abraham Lincoln	1809-1865	1861-1865
17	Andrew Johnson	1808-1875	1865-1869
18	Ulysses S. Grant	1822-1885	1869-1877

The Country's First Ladies 1830–1870

FIRST LADY	LIFETIME
Rachel Donelson Robards Jackson	1767-1828
Hannah Hoes Van Buren	1807-1819
Anna Tuthill Symmes Harrison	1775-1864
Letitia Christian Tyler	1790-1842
Julia Gardiner Tyler	1820-1889
Sarah Childress Polk	1803-1891
Margaret Mackall Smith Taylor	1788-1852
Abigail Powers Fillmore	1798-1853
Jane Means Appleton Pierce	1806-1863
Mary Todd Lincoln	1818-1882
Eliza McCardle Johnson	1810-1876
Julia Boggs Dent Grant	1826-1902

Inventions of the Era

INVENTION	INVENTOR
Reaping machine patented	Cyrus Hall McCormick
First electric clock	Carl August von Steinheil
Morse code	Samuel Morse
Combine harvester	Hiram Moore
Steam shovel	William Otis
Solar compass	William Austin Burt
Vulcanized rubber	Charles Goodyear
Grain elevator	Joseph Dart
Hand-cranked ice cream maker	Nancy Johnson
Jackhammer	Jonathan J. Couch
Potato chips	George Crum
Clothespin	David M. Smith
Mason jar	John Landis Mason
Lever-action repeating rifle	Benjamin Tyler Henry
Postcard	John P. Charlton
Barbed wire	Lucien B. Smith

Disease in America

DISEASE	YEAR
Cholera	1832
Smallpox Typhus	1837
Chlorea	1840s and 1850s
Yellow Fever	1841
Yellow Fever	1847
Yellow Fever Influenze	1850
Yellow Fever	1852

DISEASE	YEAR
Yellow Fever	1855
Smallpox	1860-1862
Typhoid Yellow Fever Scarlet Fever Cholera	1865-1873

Cholera was the bane of mid-19th century America. An outbreak in 1849 spread throughout the Mississippi river system, killing more than 4,500 in St. Louis and more than 3,000 in New Orleans. Cholera was a major killer on the Oregon, Mormon and California Trails, causing 6,000 to 12,000 deaths. It is believed more than 150,000 Americans died during the two pandemics between 1832 and 1849. So many people died on the Oregon Trail that one diarist wrote that "you couldn't walk from Scotts Bluff (Nebraska) to Fort Laramie (Wyoming) without stepping on a grave."

Popular Foods of the Era

As early as 1863, a combination of poor crops, blocked supply routes and destruction of fields by federal troops caused food riots throughout the South. In some cities, armed mobs attacked stores and warehouses.

The food fed to Civil War soldiers was sparse, frequently augmented by "liberating" chickens, fruit and vegetables from enemy farms. Soldiers most frequently ate:

- hardtack (a cracker-like biscuit)
- salt pork
- salted beef
- jerky

Canned fruit, sugar, tobacco and coffee were available only when civilian merchants were in camp.

Recipe From the Era

Potato Rolls

Four large potatoes boiled, one table-spoonful of butter, salt to the taste, half a pint of milk, half a tea-cupful of yeast, flour sufficient to form a dough. Boil the potatoes, peel and mash them, and while they are hot add the butter and salt, then pour in the milk. When the mixture is lukewarm add the yeast and flour. Knead the dough, and set it away to rise, when it is light mould out your rolls, place them on buttered tins, let them rise and bake them.

from *Arthur's Home Magazine*, volume 2-3, 1853

Popular Music of the Civil War

- "Battle Hymn of the Republic"
- "The Bonnie Blue Flag"
- "Dixie"
- "The Girl I Left Behind Me"
- "God Save the South"
- "Goober Peas"
- "I'll Take You Home Kathleen"
- "John Brown's Body"
- "Lincoln and Liberty"
- "Lorena"
- "Marching Through Georgia"
- "My Maryland"
- "The New York Volunteer"
- "The Rebel Soldier"
- "Tenting Tonight"
- "The Vacant Chair"
- "When Johnny Comes Marching Home"
- "The Yellow Rose of Texas"

Books of the Era

- *The Deerslayer* by James Fenimore Cooper, 1841
- *A Christmas Carol* by Charles Dickens, 1843
- *Jane Eyre* by Charlotte Brontë, 1847
- *Wuthering Heights* by Emily Brontë, 1847
- *Vanity Fair* by William Thackeray, 1848
- *The Scarlet Letter* by Nathaniel Hawthorne, 1850
- *David Copperfield* by Charles Dickens, 1850
- *The House of the Seven Gables* by Nathaniel Hawthorne, 1851
- *Moby-Dick* by Herman Melville, 1851
- *Silas Marner* by George Eliot, 1861
- *Alice's Adventures in Wonderland* by Lewis Carroll, 1865

Reflecting the American Ideal

Washington Irving and James Fenimore Cooper were two of the most successful fiction writers of their age. Irving created such unforgettable characters as Ichabod Crane and Rip van Winkle, while Cooper brought to life the frontier hero Leatherstocking (Hawkeye). Cooper's hero reflected the independent nature of America's frontiersmen, a theme that struck a responsive chord in his readers.

On the art front, painters such as Thomas Cole and Asher Durand established a tradition of landscape art known as the Hudson River School. They, along with the Rocky Mountain painters, saw their work as a visual expression of Manifest Destiny. Hudson River School paintings reflect the themes of discovery, exploration and settlement.

Capturing the frontier in paintings fell first to George Catlin, who traveled up the Mississippi River in 1830. For five years Catlin painted scenes from nearly 50 tribes, most of which were still untouched by European civilization. Following Catlin was Karl Bodmer, a Swiss painter who was hired by German explorer Maximilian zu Wied-Neuwied. Traveling up the Missouri River in 1832, Bodmer painted everyday life in Sioux and Mandan villages.

Most Popular Names 1861–1870

MALE	FEMALE
John	Mary
William	Ann
Charles	Elizabeth
James	Emily
George	Ellen
Frank	Sarah
Henry	Margaret
Thomas	Catherine
Joseph	Ada
Edward	Jane

1860 Federal Census

STATE	TOTAL POPULATION	AGGREGATE SLAVES
Alabama	964,201	435,080
Arkansas	435,450	111,115
California	379,994	N/A
Connecticut	460,147	N/A
Delaware	112,216	1,798
Florida	140,424	61,745
Georgia	1,057,286	462,198
Illinois	1,711,951	N/A
Indiana	1,350,428	N/A
Iowa	674,913	N/A
Kansas (territory)	107,206	2
Kentucky	1,155,684	225,483
Louisiana	708,002	331,726
Maine	628,279	N/A

STATE	TOTAL POPULATION	AGGREGATE SLAVES
Maryland	687,049	87,189
Massachusetts	1,231,066	N/A
Michigan	749,113	N/A
Minnesota	172,023	N/A
Mississippi	791,305	436,631
Missouri	1,182,012	114,931
Nebraska (territory)	28,841	15
Nevada (territory)	6,857	N/A
New Hampshire	326,073	N/A
New Jersey	672,035	18
New York	3,880,735	N/A
North Carolina	992,622	331,059
Ohio	2,339,511	N/A
Oregon	52,465	N/A
Pennsylvania	2,906,215	N/A
Rhode Island	174,620	N/A
South Carolina	703,708	402,406
Tennessee	1,109,801	275,719
Texas	604,215	182,566
Vermont	315,098	N/A
Virginia	1,596,318	490,865
Wisconsin	775,881	N/A

Top 10 U.S. Cities by Population in 1860

CITY	POPULATION
New York City	813,669
Philadelphia	565,529
Brooklyn City, New York	266,661

Baltimore	212,418
Boston	177,840
New Orleans	168,675
Cincinnati	161,044
St. Louis	160,773
Chicago	112,172
Buffalo, New York	81,129

Proportion of Blacks and Whites in the South, 1860

STATE	WHITE	BLACK	FREE BLACKS
South Carolina	42%	57%	1%
Mississippi	45%	55%	
Louisiana	50%	47%	3%
Alabama	55%	44%	1%
Florida	55%	44%	1%
Georgia	56%	44%	
Virginia	56%	39%	5%
Texas	64%	33%	3%
North Carolina	70%	30%	
Arkansas	74%	26%	
Tennessee	74%	25%	1%
Maryland	75%	13%	12%
Kentucky	80%	20%	
Delaware	81%	2%	17%
Missouri	90%	10%	

Top Immigration by Country

An immigrant entering the United States at New York City between 1855 and 1890 probably came through Castle Garden, the United States' first immigrant receiving center and the forerunner of Ellis Island. Located at the tip of Manhattan Island, near Battery Park, Castle Garden saw more than 8 million immigrants pass through its doors during the 35 years it was in operation, A total of 11 million immigrants entered the United States during this time period.

COUNTRY	1841-1850	1851-1860	1861-1870
Ireland	780,719	914,119	435,778
Germany	434,626	951,667	787,468
England	32,092	247,125	222,277
China	35	41,397	64,301
Scotland	3,712	38,331	38,769
Canada/ Newfoundland	41,723	59,309	153,878
Norway/Sweden	13,903	20,931	109,298
Switzerland	4,644	25,011	23,286
France	77,262	76,358	35,986
Belgium	5,074	4,738	6,734

★ **TRIVIA** ★ By the end of the Civil War, approximately half of the Regular Army soldiers were foreign-born, with the Irish comprising more than 20 percent.

Official Census Dates of the Era

1830-1870: June 1

Non-Population Censuses of the Era

AGRICULTURAL CENSUSES: 1850, 1860, 1870

MANUFACTURING AND INDUSTRY SCHEDULES: 1850, 1860, 1870

SLAVE SCHEDULES: 1850, 1860

MORTALITY SCHEDULES: 1850, 1860, 1870

SOCIAL STATISTICS SCHEDULES: 1850, 1860, 1870

REVOLUTIONARY WAR PENSIONERS: 1840

Colonial, Territorial and State Censuses of the Era

ALABAMA: 1850, 1855, 1866

ARIZONA: 1831 (Santa Cruz County); 1852 (Pimeria Alta); 1860; 1864; 1866

ARKANSAS: 1865

CALIFORNIA: 1834 (Santa Barbara); 1852; 1870 (San Francisco County)

COLORADO: 1861, 1866 (fragments)

FLORIDA: 1837; 1840 (military); 1845; 1855 (Marion County); 1867 (several counties)

GEORGIA: 1787–1866 (various years; fragments survive); 1835 (military pensioners); 1864 (Census for Reorganizing the Georgia Militia)

HAWAII: 1847 (foreigners); 1866

ILLINOIS: 1830-1845 (every five years, various counties); 1855; 1865

IOWA: 1836 (in Wisconsin Territory); 1838-1897 (various years and communities); 1851; 1852; 1856

KANSAS: 1857 (Shawnee tribe); 1865-1925 (every 10 years); 1855, 1856, 1857, 1858, 1859 (pensioners); 1878-1894 (Institution for the Education of the Blind)

KENTUCKY: 1859 (lawyers)

MAINE: 1837 (Bangor, Portland, unincorporated towns)

MASSACHUSETTS: 1855, 1865

MICHIGAN: 1837 (Kalamazoo County); 1845, 1854-1894 (every 10 years)

MINNESOTA: 1836 (in Wisconsin Territory); 1849; 1850; 1853 (various areas); 1855 (fragments); 1857, 1865

MISSISSIPPI: 1831 (Choctaw tribe); 1837, 1841, 1845, 1853, 1866 (various areas); 1830, 1850, 1860

MISSOURI: 1840, 1844, 1852, 1856, 1857-1858, 1868-1869

NEBRASKA: 1854, 1855, 1856, 1860, 1865, 1869

NEVADA: 1862, 1863

NEW JERSEY: 1824-1832 (Paterson); 1855, 1865

NEW MEXICO: 1750–1845 (various years and areas); 1864

NEW YORK: 1835–1865 (every 10 years)

NORTH CAROLINA: 1793–1840 (Black craftsmen); 1852 (pensioners)

NORTH DAKOTA: 1857 (Pembina County); 1855

OHIO: 1863 (African-American residents arriving between 1861 and 1863)

OREGON: 1842, 1843, 1845, 1846, 1849; 1853–1859 (every year); 1865

RHODE ISLAND: 1865

SOUTH CAROLINA: 1839 (Kershaw and Chesterfield districts); 1868, 1869

SOUTH DAKOTA: 1836 (in Wisconsin Territory); 1840 (in Iowa Territory); 1850 (Minnesota Territory); 1860, 1870

UTAH: 1852, 1856

WASHINGTON: 1857–1892 (various years and areas)

WISCONSIN: 1836–1847 (various years and counties); 1855, 1865 (fragments)

WYOMING: 1855–1865; 1869

5

Industrial Revolution, War and Depression

1870 to **1933**

About the Era

When the era began in 1870, the majority of Americans were still working on farms; by 1910, the workforce had shifted to industry. The so-called Second Industrial Revolution was underway.

The decades following the Civil War brought rapid population growth, the burgeoning of factories and a population shift from rural areas into the cities. As the United States celebrated her first 100 years as a nation, new inventions were introduced, the railroads expanded west and subways came to New York and Boston. Out West, American Indian warfare was all but over following the defeat of the 7th Cavalry at the Little Bighorn.

At the turn of the 20th century, new territories were opened to settlement, new states joined the Union and skyscrapers, like the Empire State Building, towered over the cities.

The horrors of the Civil War gave way to a brief conflict with Spain and a yearlong entry into the Great War in Europe. It was an age of optimism, marked by growth, progress and expansion. But just when it seemed that America's growth was unstoppable, the stock market crash of 1929 sent the country spiraling into what would forever be known as the Great Depression. The stage was now set for a New Deal.

Events That Shaped the Era

1871 Hundreds die in the Great Chicago Fire; other fires rage in Peshtigo, Wisconsin, and in Michigan

1872 Montgomery Ward founded

1873 Economic Panic of 1873

U.S. Army Signal Corps issues its first hurricane warning

1873–1877 Swarms of locusts damage $200 million in crops in Colorado, Kansas, Minnesota, Nebraska, Missouri and elsewhere.

1874 Founding of Woman's Christian Temperance Union

1875 Sioux ordered to vacate Powder River Country

1876 Battle of the Little Bighorn

Philadelphia Centennial

Alexander Graham Bell patents the telephone

1876 Train wreck near Ashtabula, Ohio, claims 97 lives

1877 Chinese riots in San Francisco

1881 President James Garfield assassinated

Andrew Carnegie offers to build libraries for every American city

Hurricane hits Georgia and the Carolinas, killing 700

1882 Chinese Exclusion Act

1883 Railroad establishes national time zones

1884 February 19, tornadoes kill hundreds in Southern states

1887 Florida establishes law segregating railroad travel

1888 January blizzard kills hundreds in Montana, Dakota Territory and Nebraska; 400 die in the Northeast during the Great Blizzard

1889 Oklahoma opened to land rush

Heavy rains collapse a dam at Johnstown, Pennsylvania, killing more than 2,000

1890 Massacre at Wounded Knee

Mississippi becomes first state to adopt literacy test to disenfranchise black voters

1897 Boston builds first American subway

1898 Spanish-American War

1898 Avalanche near Sheep Camp, Alaska, is the deadliest event of the Klondike Gold Rush

1900 Hurricane in Galveston, Texas, kills more than 6,000

1901 Theodore Roosevelt becomes president upon assassination of William McKinley

1906 San Francisco earthquake and ensuing fire kills thousands

1912 Woodrow Wilson elected president

Sinking of the Titanic

1914 Panama Canal opens

World War I begins

1917 United States enters World War I

1919 Great Boston Molasses Flood kills 21 and injures 150

Beginning of Prohibition

1920 19th Amendment ensures woman suffrage

1921 Immigration Act

1922–1923 Teapot Dome Scandal

1925 Tornado kills nearly 700 in Illinois, Indiana and Missouri

1927 Floods cause devastation and social upheaval along the Mississippi River

1928 Herbert Hoover elected president

1929 Stock market crash

1930 Midwest drought begins

1933 Franklin Roosevelt becomes president

End of Prohibition

11 States Join the Union

NUMBER BY ADMISSION	STATE	DATE ADMITTED	ORIGIN
38	Colorado	August 1, 1876	Colorado Territory
39	North Dakota	November 2, 1889	Dakota Territory
40	South Dakota	November 2, 1889	Dakota Territory
41	Montana	November 8, 1889	Montana Territory
42	Washington	November 11, 1889	Washington Territory
43	Idaho	July 3, 1890	Idaho Territory
44	Wyoming	July 10, 1890	Wyoming Territory
45	Utah	January 4, 1896	Utah Territory
46	Oklahoma	November 16, 1907	Oklahoma Territory and Indian Territory
47	New Mexico	January 6, 1912	New Mexico Territory
48	Arizona	February 14, 1912	Arizona Territory

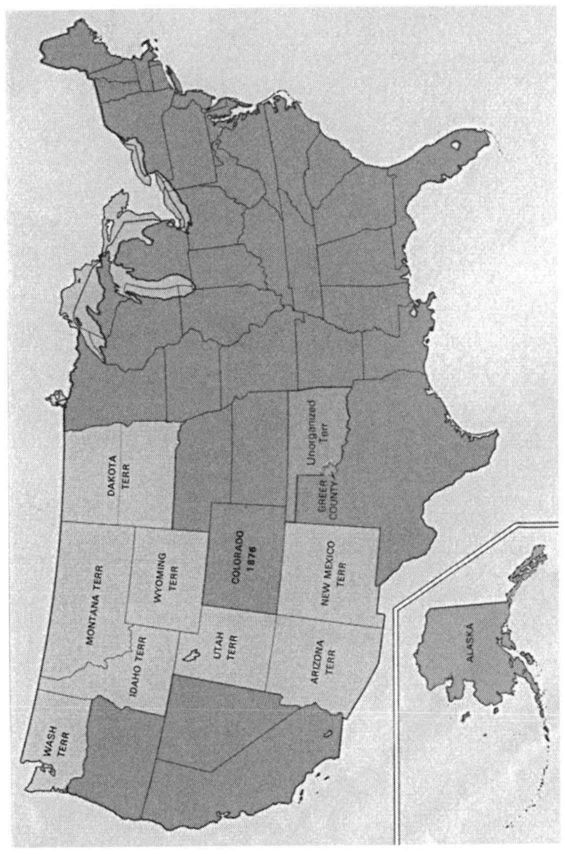

Territorial Growth, 1880
Courtesy of the University of Texas Libraries, The University of Texas at Austin

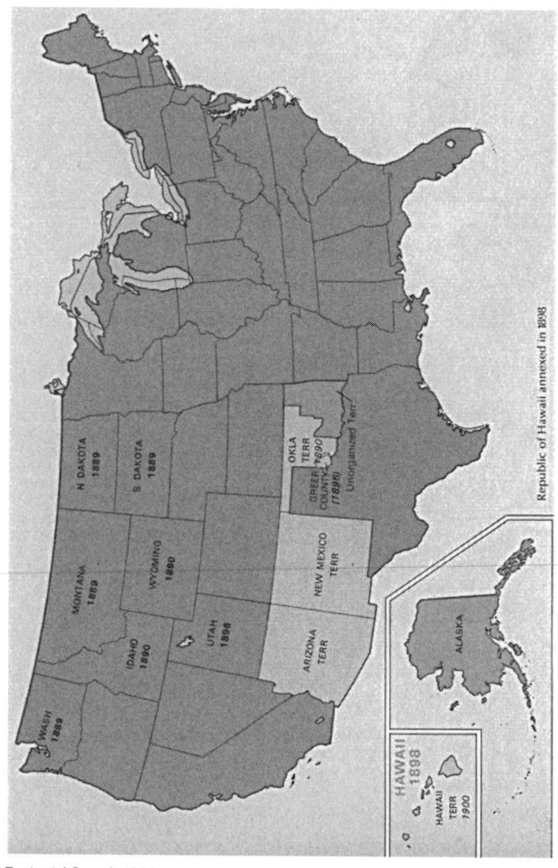

Territorial Growth, 1900
Courtesy of the University of Texas Libraries, The University of Texas at Austin

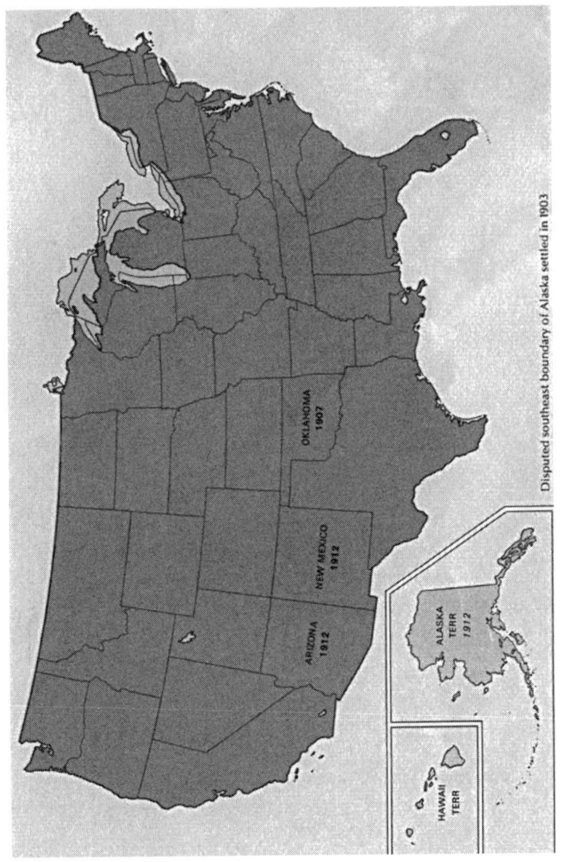

Territorial Growth, 1920
Courtesy of the University of Texas Libraries, The University of Texas at Austin

Land Rush!

Present-day Oklahoma was once a part of Indian Territory; in 1887, the Dawes Act divided the land into allotments for American Indians but reserved a portion for the federal government. Two million acres in Oklahoma Territory not assigned to any tribe, came under the provisions of the Homestead Act in 1889, sparking two of the wildest land rushes in American history. The first was on April 22, 1889, when thousands of claimants staked out claims in just a few hours. By the end of the day, two tent cities arose, Guthrie and Oklahoma City with 10,000 residents each.

The second land grab in Oklahoma Territory took place on September 16, 1893, when the Cherokee Strip was opened to settlement. Located in the northern part of Oklahoma Territory, the strip was also claimed under the Homestead Act.

Major American Wars of the Era

INDIAN WARS, 1866-1890: While skirmishes between American Indians and Europeans had been taking place over decades, the era from 1866 to 1890 saw an escalation that all but eradicated the Indian's way of life. The chart describes major events during this conflict.

NAME	DATE	PLACE	CAUSE	OUTCOME	TRIBES
Dakota War	Summer and fall, 1862	Minnesota	Failure of the government to provide promised provisions	300 warriors sentenced to hang; Lincoln commuted all but 38.	Santee Sioux
Fetterman Massacre	December 21, 1866	Wyoming Territory	Indian resistance to invasion of territory along the Bozeman Trail	Capt. Fetterman and all of his men were killed in an ambush near Fort Phil Kearny.	Lakota Sioux, Northern Cheyenne, Northern Arapaho

Washita Massacre	November 27, 1868	Present-day Oklahoma	Gen. Sheridan's winter campaign against Cheyenne	Col. Custer attacked the village of peace chief Black Kettle, killing 103 women, old men and children.	Cheyenne
Modoc War	1872–1873	Southern Oregon, Northern California	Attempt to hold off European encroachment on Modoc territory	Capt. Jack and his three lead warriors were hanged at Fort Klamath; the remainder of the band were sent to Oklahoma.	Modoc
Red River War	1874–1875	Texas	Attempt of the Army to remove Comanche, Kiowa, Southern Cheyenne and Arapaho to Indian Territory	Quanah Parker and his band of Quahadi Comanche surrendered at Fort Sill; Texas Panhandle was opened to settlement.	Comanche, Kiowa, Southern Cheyenne, Arapaho
Battle of the Rosebud	June 17, 1876	Montana Territory	Army ordered to force all "hostiles" onto reservations	Gen. Crook's forces were taken by surprise and withdrew.	Sioux, Cheyenne
Battle of the Little Bighorn	June 25, 1876	Montana Territory	Army ordered to force all "hostiles" onto reservations	Custer and 250 of his men were killed.	Sioux, Cheyenne, Arapaho; Crow scouted for Custer
Nez Perce War	1877	Pacific Northwest	Nez Perce refused to give up their ancestral lands and move to a reservation	Chief Joseph, the principal chief, surrendered to Gen. O.O. Howard.	Nez Perce; Lakota and Cheyenne scouted for the Army
Apache Wars	1870s–1880s	Arizona	Apache raids on Mexican and European settlers	Geronimo surrendered and was sent to Florida.	Various bands of Apache
Wounded Knee Massacre	December 29, 1890	South Dakota	Indians who had surrendered were killed when soldiers thought they were planning to rebel	Approximately 300 Sioux were killed, including men, women and children.	Miniconjous Sioux

SPANISH-AMERICAN WAR, 1898: Conflict between the United States and Spain over U.S. interests in Cuba. Spurred by the sinking of the *U.S.S. Maine* in Havana Harbor.

WORLD WAR I 1917-1918: Called the Great War, World War I started in Europe in 1914 and ended in 1918, with U.S. involvement beginning in 1917. America first pursued a policy of nonintervention but two events propelled the United States into war. One was the sinking of seven U.S. merchant ships by German U-boats; the second was the release of the Zimmermann Telegram, in which Germany urged Mexico to join the war against the United States and, in return, Germany would fund Mexican efforts as well as help them reclaim Texas, Arizona and New Mexico. About 2.8 million American men were drafted during the war.

The Wild West

After the Civil War, Americans poured onto the Great Plains, building farms and ranches in territories that previously had been home to great herds of buffalo and American Indian nomads. A culture clash was unavoidable; buffalo were hunted almost to extinction and the Indians were forced onto reservations. As one culture faded, another grew—that of the wild west cowboy. Showmen like Buffalo Bill Cody fed the country's hunger for entertainment filled with wild Indians and trick roping cowhands. Cattle, which had bred unchecked in Texas throughout the Civil War, were round up and driven to the great railheads like Dodge City, Kansas. Although short-lived, the wild west was filled with colorful characters who live on in legend, like Cody, Wyatt Earp, Doc Holliday and the Clanton gang.

The Industrial Revolution

The first Industrial Revolution (1750-1850) was fueled by the introduction of steam power, which powered machinery and accounted for a dramatic increase in production. The second

Industrial Revolution began about 1850, with steam-powered ships, railroads and electrical power generation. However, a major factor in the second phase of industrial growth in the United States was the ability to convert wrought iron into steel in large quantities. By the end of the 20th century, petroleum refining reduced the need for coal, thus widening the potential for industrialization.

Between 1870 and 1910, the output of coal increased from 20 million tons to 417 million tons; at the same time, copper production rose from 14,112 tons to 544,119 tons.

In 1870, the majority of the labor force was engaged in agriculture; by 1910 labor had shifted to industry and non-agricultural jobs. By 1900, women made up more than one-quarter of the non-farm labor force.

Industrial Revolution Milestones

1870s Carnegie launches modern steel industry

New textile mills flourish in the South

1880s Electrification transforms city life

1882 First continuous process mill for oatmeal

1887 American Federation of Labor founded

1890 United States surpasses Britain in iron and steel output

Beginning of era of farm prosperity

1900 Immigrants dominate factory work

Government regulates railroads

1913 Ford builds first automobile assembly line

★ **TRIVIA** ★ In 1870 there were 53,000 miles of railroad track; in 1890, 167,000. Most of the growth took place in the South and west of the Mississippi.

Leisure Time

With industrialization came more leisure time for more Americans. For the first time, Americans had the chance to have a life outside of work. Included in their new free time were:

- baseball games
- radio dramas
- movie theaters

The Roaring Twenties

The early 1920s marked a period of economic prosperity, accompanied by a boom in art, culture and music. "Flappers" changed women's styles, jazz became a favorite and Art Deco inspired everything from art to architecture. At the same time, the enactment of Prohibition gave rise to gangsters, such as Al Capone, who smuggled liquor across the Canadian-U.S. border. This period of boom was short-lived as the Black Tuesday stock market crash of October 29, 1929, sent the country spiraling into the Great Depression.

Great Depression

From 1929 to approximately 1933, the world underwent a severe economic depression. Beginning with the Black Tuesday (October 29, 1929) stock market crash, the depression quickly spread from the United States to around the world. Unemployment rose to 25 percent and crop prices fell by 60 percent. Hundreds of thousands of Americans became homeless, setting up tent cities called "Hoovervilles," named for President Herbert Hoover. Although Black Tuesday marked the start of the Great Depression, other factors helped fuel the downturn, including over-investing under-consumption and a decrease in international trade.

The Most Famous Kidnapping of the Era

On March 1, 1932, 20-month-old Charles Augustus Lindbergh, Jr., son of the famous aviator, was kidnapped from his second floor nursery at the family's home near Hopewell, New Jersey. The kidnapping drew nationwide attention and involved investigative teams from local, state and national agencies, including the FBI. The Lindbergh baby's body was discovered in May 1932; the kidnapper, Bruno Richard Hauptmann, a German immigrant was tried, found guilty and sentenced to death.

Famous People of the Era

SITTING BULL (c.1831-1890): Spiritual leader of the Hunkpapa Sioux

CRAZY HORSE (c.1840-1877): War leader of the Oglala Sioux

GEN. GEORGE ARMSTRONG CUSTER (1839-1876): Civil War general, died at the Battle of the Little Bighorn

JOHN "DOC" HOLLIDAY (1851-1887): Gambler and gunfighter, friend of Wyatt Earp; participated in the gunfight at the O.K. Corral

WYATT EARP (1848-1929): Lawman who served in Wichita and Dodge City, Kansas, later in Tombstone, Arizona

WILLIAM HENRY MCCARTY, JR. "BILLY THE KID" (1859-1881): Gunman and frontier outlaw in the Southwest

WILLIAM F. "BUFFALO BILL" CODY (1846-1917): Army scout and buffalo hunter and showman famous for his Wild West show

ANNIE OAKLEY (1860–1926): Sharpshooter in Buffalo Bill's Wild West show

JOSEPH LISTER (1827–1912): Physician and pioneer of the concept of antiseptic surgery

THEODORE ROOSEVELT (1858–1919): Twenty-sixth president of the United States and founder of the "Bull Moose" party

THOMAS EDISON (1847-1931): American inventor of the phonograph and light bulb

ANDREW CARNEGIE (1835–1919): Steel magnate and one of the most influential philanthropists of his day

JOHN D. ROCKEFELLER (1839–1937): Oil millionaire and philanthropist, the founder of the Standard Oil Company

JOHN JACOB ASTOR IV (1864–1912): American millionaire, veteran of the Spanish-American War, died on the *Titanic*

MARGARET "MOLLY" BROWN (1867–1932): Socialite, daughter of Irish immigrants; survived the sinking of the *Titanic*, earning her the nickname "The Unsinkable Molly Brown"

SIR ARTHUR CONAN DOYLE (1859–1930): Author of the Sherlock Holmes mysteries

CHARLIE CHAPLIN (1889–1977): Actor and director during the era of silent films

TYRUS "TY" COBB "THE GEORGIA PEACH" (1886–1961): Set 90 records during his career as a professional baseball player

GEORGE HERMAN "BABE" RUTH (1895-1948): Professional baseball player who was considered one of the best home run hitters in the history of the game

CHARLES LINDBERGH (1902-1974): First man to fly solo across the Atlantic Ocean

AMELIA EARHART (1897-1937): Aviation pioneer, first aviatrix to fly solo across the Atlantic Ocean

BARON MANFRED VON RICHTHOFEN (1892-1918): The Red Baron, German fighter pilot during World War I

WILLIAM "BILLY" MITCHELL (1879-1936): American general who foresaw the importance of air power; commanded all air combat units in World War I

F. SCOTT FITZGERALD (1896-1940): Author of *The Great Gatsby*, member of the "lost generation" of writers who came of age during World War I

EDWARD "DUKE" ELLINGTON (1899-1974): Big band leader and famous jazz musician

ALPHONSE "AL" CAPONE (1899-1947): Gangster who controlled prostitution, smuggling and gambling in Chicago

ELIOTT NESS (1903-1957): Federal agent best known for his efforts to enforce Prohibition in Chicago during the 1920s; leader of the famous group of agents known as The Untouchables

HERBERT HOOVER (1874-1964): Thirty-first president of the United States; the Great Depression struck just months into his presidency

The Country's Presidents 1870–1933

NUMBER BY DATE IN OFFICE	PRESIDENT	LIFETIME	YEARS IN OFFICE
18	Ulysses S. Grant	1822-1885	1869-1877
19	Rutherford B. Hayes	1822-1893	1877-1881
20	James A. Garfield	1831-1881	March 4-September 19, 1881
21	Chester A. Arthur	1829-1886	1881-1885
22	Grover Cleveland	1837-1908	1885-1889
23	Benjamin Harrison	1833-1901	1889-1893
	Grover Cleveland	1837-1908	1893-1897
	William McKinley	1843-1901	1897-1901
	Theodore Roosevelt	1858-1919	1901-1909
	William Howard Taft	1857-1930	1909-1913
28	Woodrow Wilson	1856-1924	1913-1921
29	Warren G. Harding	1865-1923	1921-1923
30	Calvin Coolidge	1872-1933	1923-1929
31	Herbert Hoover	1874-1964	1929-1933

Speak Softly and Carry a Big Stick

Theodore Roosevelt was a larger-than-life American president who lived life to the fullest. He was a hunter, explorer, rancher, cowboy, reformer, conservationist, author and the first American to win the Noble Peace Prize. A volunteer Rough Rider in the Spanish-American War, "T.R." went on to become assistant secretary of the Navy, vice president and then president. During his presidency, Roosevelt established what would become the Wildlife Refuge System. He was also responsible for passing the Antiquities Act in 1906, which allowed the president to preserve historic sites as national monuments. A believer in a strong national defense, he was known for his "speak softly and carry a big stick" policies.

The Country's First Ladies 1870–1933

FIRST LADY	LIFETIME
Julia Dent Grant	1826-1902
Lucy Ware Webb Hayes	1831-1889
Lucretia Rudolph Garfield	1832-1918
Ellen Lewis Herndon Arthur	1837-1880
Frances Folsom Cleveland	1864-1947
Caroline Lavinia Scott Harrison	1832-1892
Ida Saxton McKinley	1847-1907
Edith Kermit Carow Roosevelt	1861-1948
Helen Herron Taft	1861-1943
Ellen Axson Wilson	1860-1914
Edith Bolling Galt Wilson	1872-1961
Florence Kling Harding	1860-1924
Grace Anna Goodhue Coolidge	1879-1957
Lou Henry Hoover	1874-1944

"Give Me Your Tired, Your Poor/ Your Huddled Masses Yearning to Breathe Free"

Dedicated on October 28, 1886, the Statue of Liberty was a gift to the United States from the people of France. Lady Liberty has become an enduring symbol of freedom to people around the world. The statue measures 305 feet, 1 inch from the base of the pedestal to the tip of the torch and has a total weight of 450,000 pounds.

Inventions of the Era

YEAR	INVENTION
1872	Railway air brake
1872	Diner
1873	Silo
1873	Jeans
1874	QWERTY (typewriter keyboard layout)
1877	Phonograph
1879	Cash register
1881	Metal detector
1888	AC motor
1891	Ferris wheel
1891	Zipper
1892	Tractor
1894	Mousetrap
1900	Thumbtack
1901	Assembly line
1901	Safety razor
1902	Teddy bear
1903	Airplane
1919	Pop-up toaster
1920	Polygraph
1920	Broadcast of first radio news program
1928	Iron lung

America Takes to the Skies

On October 24, 1911, at Kitty Hawk, North Carolina, Orville Wright established a new world record in soaring by flying for nine minutes and 45 seconds in a 50 mile-per-hour wind. Experiments by Orville and his brother, Wilbur, resulted in the world's first powered-controlled flight. Kitty Hawk, located on North Carolina's Outer Banks, was a perfect test ground because of its steady winds.

Two Deadly Epidemics of the Early 20th Century

POLIO: In 1916, an official announcement declared the existence of a polio epidemic. In America, more than 27,000 cases and 6,000 deaths were attributed to polio in 1916. Names and addresses of infected individuals were published daily in the newspaper. This epidemic led to a panic, with the closure of theaters and public gatherings. Water fountains, amusement parks and swimming pools were avoided.

SPANISH FLU (1918-1919): This was the worst pandemic of the 20th century. Up to 40 percent of the worldwide population became ill, with more than 50 million deaths.

Epidemics

DISEASE	YEAR
Influenza	1873-1875
Smallpox	1876
Yellow Fever	1878
Typhoid	1885
Yellow Fever	1886
Bubonic Plague (San Francisco)	1900-1904
Polio	1916
Spanish Influenza	1918-1919

Popular Foods of the Era

- Chicken Curry
- Orange Budding
- Dutch Flummery
- Calf's Feet Jelly
- French Milk Porridge
- Russian Seed
- Suffolk Dumplings
- Fried Herring
- Green Bean Pudding
- Snow Cream
- Plum Cake

Recipes From the Era

Rice Flummery

Boil with a pint of new milk, and a bit of lemon-peel, and cinnamon: mix with a little cold milk, as much rice flour, as will make the whole of a good consistence: sweeten, and add a spoonful of peach-water, or a bitter almond beaten. Boil it, observing it does not burn. Pour it into a shape or pint basin, taking out the spice. When cold, turn the flummery in a dish, and serve with cream, milk or custard around: or put a teaspoonful of cream into a half a pint of new milk, a glass of raising wine, a little sugar, and a squeeze of lemon.

From *The Southern Cookbook* by S. Thomas Bivins, 1912

Turn-of-the-Century Recipe for Fudge

2 cups sugar
1 teaspoon vanilla
3 tablespoon butter
½ cup milk
2 oz. chocolate

Directions:
Put all of the ingredients except vanilla in an agate saucepan and boil, stirring seldom until a ball will form when placed in cold water. Flavor, set the pan into cold water and beat til candy is creamy, or let it stand 10–15 min. and then beat the candy. Pour into pan and when cold cut into squares.

From *The Practical Cookbook: A Book of Economical Recipes* by Margaret W. Howard, 1917.

Prices During the Era

YEAR	MILK (PER GALLON)	HOUSE	AVERAGE ANNUAL INCOME
1880	16 cents	$4,500	$480
1885	17 cents	$5,500	$540
1890	17 cents	$5,800	$660
1895	20 cents	$4,850	$640
1900	30 cents	$4,000	$637
1905	29 cents	$4,000	$862
1910	33 cents	$4,800	$963
1915	36 cents	$4,800	$1,076
1920	58 cents	$6,296	$1,130
1925	56 cents	$7,809	$1,324
1930	56 cents	$7,146	$1,612

Popular Songs of World War I

- "For Me and My Gal"
- "Hello, Who's Your Lady Friend?"
- "I Wonder Who's Kissing Her Now"
- "If You Were the Only Girl in the World"
- "It's a Long Way to Tipperary"
- "Keep the Home Fires Burning"

- "Lloyd George's Beer"
- "Lorraine (My Beautiful Alsace Lorraine)"
- "Over There"
- "Pack Up Your Troubles in Your Old Kit Bag "
- "The Rose of No Man's Land"
- "They Didn't Believe Me"

Books of the Era

- *Ramona* by Helen Hunt Jackson, 1884
- *Lord Jim* by Joseph Conrad, 1900
- *The Wonderful Wizard of Oz* by L. Frank Baum, 1900
- *Kim* by Rudyard Kipling, 1901
- *Heart of Darkness* by Joseph Conrad, 1902
- *The Hound of the Baskervilles* by Sir Arthur Conan Doyle, 1902
- *The Call of the Wild* by Jack London, 1903
- *The Jungle* by Upton Sinclair, 1906
- *Peter Pan in Kensington Gardens* by J. M. Barrie, 1906
- *Anne of Green Gables* by Lucy Montgomery, 1908
- *The Wind in the Willows* by Kenneth Grahame, 1908
- *Tarzan of the Apes* by Edgar Rice Burroughs, 1912
- *A Portrait of the Artist as a Young Man* by James Joyce, 1916
- *The Age of Innocence* by Edith Wharton, 1920
- *Babbitt* by Sinclair Lewis, 1922
- *Mrs. Dalloway* by Virginia Woolf, 1925
- *All Quiet on the Western Front* by Erich Maria Remarque, 1928

Going to the Movies

Movies, as we know them, began early in the 20th century with sound being introduced in the 1920s and Technicolor in the 1930s. Attendance dropped off during the Great Depression, causing theater owners to drop ticket prices. In 1930, Greta Garbo's first talking picture, "Anna Christie," was released. In the same year, Marlene Dietrich starred in "The Blue Angel."

Academy Award Winners

YEAR	MOVIE	BEST ACTRESS	BEST ACTOR
1928	"Wings"	Janet Gaynor	Emil Jannings
1929	"The Broadway Melody"	Mary Pickford	Warner Baxter
1930	"All Quiet on the Western Front"	Norma Shearer	George Arliss
1931	"Cimarron"	Marie Dressler	Lionel Barrymore
1932	"Grand Hotel"	Helen Hayes	Wallace Beery & Fredric Marsh
1933	"Cavalcade"	Katharine Hepburn	Charles Laughton

Most Popular Names 1880

MALE	FEMALE
William	Mary
John	Ann
Charles	Elizabeth
James	Emily
George	Ada
Henry	Ellen
Joseph	Margaret
Frank	Catherine
Thomas	Sarah
Edward	Minnie

Most Popular Names 1920

MALE	FEMALE
John	Mary
William	Helen
Robert	Ann
James	Margaret

MALE	FEMALE
Joseph	Elizabeth
Charles	Dorothy
George	Ruth
Harry	Ellen
Edward	Lou
Frank	Catherine

Median Age at Marriage (Estimate)

YEAR	WOMEN	MEN
1890	22	26
1900	22	26
1910	22	25
1920	21	25
1930	21	24

Total Population of the United States, 1900–1930

YEAR	POPULATION
1900	76,212,168
1905	83,822,000 estimate
1910	92,228,496
1915	100,546,000 estimate
1920	106,021,537
1925	115,829,000 estimate
1930	123,202,624

★ **TRIVIA** ★ 1918 was the only year that population growth decreased.

Top 10 U.S. Cities by Population in 1870

CITY	POPULATION
New York City	942,292
Philadelphia	674,022
Brooklyn, New York	396,099
St. Louis	310,864
Chicago	298,977
Baltimore	267,354
Boston	250,526
Cincinnati	216,239
New Orleans	191,418
San Francisco	149,473

Top 10 U.S. Cities by Population in 1930

CITY	POPULATION
New York City	6,930,446
Chicago	3,376,438
Philadelphia	1,950,961
Detroit	1,568,662
Los Angeles	1,238,048
Cleveland	900,429
St. Louis	821,960
Baltimore	804,874
Boston	781,188
Pittsburgh	669,817

Two Labor Forces Come to America

With the rise of industrialization, rail lines were built along the U.S.-Mexican border, which allowed copper mines to open in Arizona, cotton to be cultivated in Texas and large-scale orchards to be established in California. These new industries in sparsely populated areas needed labor. Because the U.S.-Mexican border was open until 1917, no one knows exactly how many Hispanics migrated into the new workforce; however, in Texas the Hispanic population increased from 20,000 in 1850 to 165,000 in 1900.

Many of the Mexicans came to the United States as short-term or seasonal labor, although those who stayed established large Mexican communities, such as Tucson, Arizona. In other cities, immigrants lived in *barrios*—the equivalent of a Mexican ghetto, where they worked the most difficult and lowest-paying jobs.

California's gold rush of 1849 attracted Chinese immigrants by the thousands, where they eventually made up one-quarter of the state's labor force. Once in California, most Chinese immigrants came under the control of the Six Companies, a loose confederation of Chinese merchants in San Francisco. When gold mining played out, Chinese laborers went to work for the Central Pacific Railroad as it laid track as part of the transcontinental railroad system. Although some Chinese went to other states upon completion of the railroad, most stayed in California; the 1880 census showed that nearly three-quarters of the immigrants remained in the Golden State.

In the late 1870s, violent anti-Chinese riots took place in San Francisco, led by an Irish teamster named Denis Kearney. Finally, in 1882, the Chinese Exclusion Act was passed, barring entry of Chinese laborers into the United States.

Ellis Island Opens

In 1892, a new immigration station opened in New York City at Ellis Island. From 1892 to 1954, more than 12 million immigrants entered the United States through Ellis Island. Prior to 1890, individual states regulated immigration into the United States, with Castle Garden being the New York entryway. While Ellis Island was the main immigration station of the era, immigrants also entered through other ports such as San Francisco, Baltimore and New Orleans.

Top 10 Immigration by Country 1871–1880

COUNTRY	IMMIGRANTS
Germany	718,182
England	437,706
Ireland	436,871
China	123,201
Sweden	115,922
Norway	95,323
Scotland	87,564
Austria-Hungary	72,969
France	72,206
Italy	55,759

Top 10 Immigration by Country 1921–1930

COUNTRY	IMMIGRANTS
Italy	455,315
Germany	412,202
Poland	227,734
Ireland	210,024
Scotland	159,781
England	157,420
Czechoslovakia	102,194
Sweden	68,531
Romania	67,646
USSR	61,742

Official Census Dates of the Era

1870: June 1
1880: June 1
1890: June 2
1900: June 1
1910: April 15
1920: January 1
1930: April 1

Non-Population Censuses of the Era

SCHEDULES OF DEFECTIVE, DEPENDENT AND DELINQUENT CLASSES : 1880

AGRICULTURAL CENSUSES: 1880

MANUFACTURING AND INDUSTRY SCHEDULES: 1880

MORTALITY SCHEDULES: 1880, 1885 (some areas), 1900 (Minnesota only)

U.S. STATE/TERRITORIAL CENSUS: 1885 (some areas)

SOCIAL STATISTICS SCHEDULES: 1885

INDIAN SCHEDULES: 1880, 1900, 1910

INDIAN RESERVATION CENSUSES: 1885–1940

INDIAN SCHOOL CENSUSES: 1910–1939

CIVIL WAR VETERANS SCHEDULES: 1890 (extant for half of Kentucky and states alphabetically following)

SCHEDULES OF MILITARY PERSONNEL ON BASES AND VESSELS (INCLUDING OVERSEAS): 1900, 1910, 1920

SCHEDULES OF MERCHANT SEAMEN ON VESSELS: 1930

Colonial, Territorial and State Censuses of the Era

ALABAMA: 1907 (Confederate veterans); 1921 (Confederate pensioners)

ALASKA: 1878 (Aleutian Islands); 1879, 1881 (Sitka); 1885 (Cape Smith, Point Barrow); 1890-1895 (Pribiloff Islands); 1904-1907, 1914, 1917 (St. Paul and St. George islands); 1890 (Naval Veterans)

ARIZONA: 1882 (several counties); 1883 (Pensioners on the Roll)

ARKANSAS: 1911

CALIFORNIA: 1870 (San Francisco County)

COLORADO: 1885; 1898 (Volunteers for the Spanish-American War); 1904-1908 (Ute Census of Navajo Springs)

CONNECTICUT: 1917 (males of military service age, some women)

FLORIDA: 1875 (Alachua County); 1885; 1895 (Nassau County)

HAWAII: 1878 (Hawaii, Maui, Oahu); 1890; 1896 (Honolulu)

ILLINOIS: 1880 (Cook County)

INDIANA: 1880 (Clark County)

IOWA: 1885, 1895, 1905, 1915, 1925

KANSAS: 1875–1925 (every 10 years); 1873-on (various years and areas); 1883 (pensioners); 1878–1894 (Institution for the Education of the Blind)

LOUISIANA: 1911 (Confederate soldiers and widows)

MICHIGAN: 1854-1894 (every 10 years); 1883 (pensioners); 1894 (veterans)

MINNESOTA: 1875, 1885, 1895, 1905

MISSOURI: 1873, 1876 (fragments); 1880, 1881

MONTANA: 1883 (pensioners); 1897–1898 (Blackfeet tribe)

NEBRASKA: 1885; 1893 (veterans)

NEVADA: 1875

NEW JERSEY: 1875, 1885, 1895, 1905, 1915

NEW MEXICO: 1885

NEW YORK: 1875, 1892, 1905, 1915, 1925

NORTH DAKOTA: 1885–1939 (various Indian reservations); 1915, 1925

OKLAHOMA: 1880, 1890, 1896 (Cherokee tribe); 1890; 1907 (Seminole County)

OREGON: 1875-1905 (every 10 years)

PENNSYLVANIA: 1902 (children in soldier's orphan schools)

RHODE ISLAND: 1875, 1885, 1905, 1915, 1925, 1935

SOUTH CAROLINA: 1875 (several counties)

SOUTH DAKOTA: 1870, 1880 (Dakota Territory); 1885-1925 (every 10 years); 1885-1940 (Indian census, various years)

UTAH: 1872, 1896

VIRGINIA: 1890 (Union veterans census of southwest Virginia)

WASHINGTON: 1857-1892 (various years and areas)

WISCONSIN: 1875-1905 (every 10 years)

WYOMING: 1875-1905 (every 10 years); 1869; 1878 (Cheyenne)

6

New Deal and World War II

1933 to **1945**

About the Era

When Franklin Delano Roosevelt ("FDR") entered the White House in 1933, America was in the depths of the Great Depression. Roosevelt quickly enacted legislation to get the American economy moving again. While his efforts to rebuild the country were successful, he wasn't able to keep a neutral United States out of World War II. With the December 7, 1941, attack on Pearl Harbor, Hawaii, the United States entered four years of war.

Although it was one of the most difficult periods in American history, the war years united the country, helped to break down racial barriers, added women to the workforce and increased factory production like no time in the past. In Dickens' words, "it was the best of times, it was the worst of times."

Events That Shaped the Era

1930s Drought and over farming in the Southern Plains create "Dust Bowl" storms; displaced farmers leave Oklahoma, Texas, Kansas and other states

1933 Germany leaves the League of Nations

Banking crisis

FDR's first Fireside Chat

Prohibition repealed

1936 Mussolini conquered Ethiopia

Roosevelt reelected to second term

1937 Ohio River reaches record flood levels

1938 Orson Welles' *The War of the Worlds* airs

Hurricane strikes New York and New England

Germany invades Austria, annexing it to the Third Reich

1939 Germany invades Poland in an all-out attack called a *blitzkrieg*

1940 Pact created between Germany, Italy and Japan—the Axis Powers

Roosevelt reelected to third term

1940-1941 The Blitz: Sustained bombing of Britain and Northern Ireland; London suffered 57 consecutive nights of bombing.

1941 Lend-Lease Act passed, permitted shipment of materials to countries the United States deemed vital to its security

Japan launches surprise attack on Pearl Harbor, Hawaii United States enters World War II

1942 Allies suffer losses including Wake Island, Guam, Philippines, Singapore, Burma and Hong Kong

Bataan Death March, forced march of U.S. and Filipino soldiers who surrendered at Corregidor; the march resulted in the death of 10,000 POWs

Japanese-Americans living within 200 miles of the Pacific were forced into relocation camps

Battle of Midway and Coral Sea halts Japanese advance in the Pacific

Battle of Guadalcanal

Battle of Stalingrad, resulted in loss of 750,000 Soviet troops

Women recruited for war effort

1942–1946 Rationing

1943 Allied forces land in Sicily

1944 Rome falls to the Allies

D-Day commences

Roosevelt reelected to fourth term

1945 Battles of Iwo Jima and Okinawa

Soviet troops enter Berlin

Roosevelt's death

Germany surrenders (May 7)

Atomic bombs dropped on Hiroshima and Nagasaki, Japan.

General Douglas MacArthur presides over the signing of Japanese surrender documents (September 2)

States Admitted to the Union

No states were admitted to the Union during this time period. It wasn't until 1959 that the last two states were admitted—Alaska on January 3, and Hawaii on August 21.

The New Deal: An Era of Recovery

When elected president in 1932, FDR offered the American people a "New Deal"—federally funded programs of economic relief and recovery. During the first 100 days of his presidency, Roosevelt introduced legislation to stimulate the economy and aid victims of the Great Depression. Programs included:

CIVILIAN CONSERVATION CORPS (CCC): The CCC put thousands of men to work on projects in national parks, forests and public lands; 250,000 men lived in CCC camps across the country. Some buildings constructed by the CCC are still standing in various locations around the country.

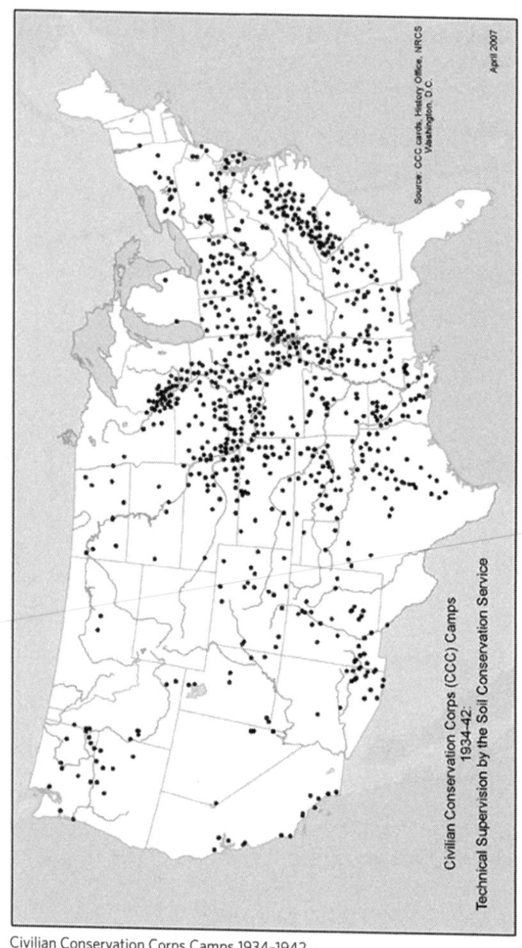

Civilian Conservation Corps Camps 1934–1942
Courtesy of the University of Texas Libraries, The University of Texas at Austin

NATIONAL RECOVERY ACT (NRA) ESTABLISHED THE PUBLIC WORKS ADMINISTRATION (PWA): Set minimum wages and maximum working hours; allowed collective bargaining

AGRICULTURAL ADJUSTMENT ADMINISTRATION: A program of federal subsidies to farmers, created an allotment system for seven major commodities: corn, wheat, cotton, rice, peanuts, tobacco and milk

TENNESSEE VALLEY AUTHORITY (TVA): Built dams, hydroelectric plants and roads in the poorest states

FEDERAL EMERGENCY RELIEF ADMINISTRATION: Gave federal money to states for relief programs

WORKS PROGRESS ADMINISTRATION (WPA): Established in 1935; over an eight-year period, the WPA put 8.5 million people to work; projects included the Federal Writers' Program and the Federal Art Program

BANKING ACT OF 1935: Consolidated government control over banks; a reorganized system placed control of interest rates at the federal level

HOME OWNERS' LOAN CORPORATION: Refinanced home mortgages threatened by foreclosures

SOCIAL SECURITY ACT: Introduced in 1935, created old-age pension and retirement funds through payroll taxes

SECURITIES AND EXCHANGE COMMISSION: Established in 1934 to stop insider trading and other stock market abuses

The Dust Bowl

The Dust Bowl of the 1930s was the result of sustained drought and over-plowing of fields in the Great Plains. As the drought continued, the ground died off and no longer held down the top soil. As wind whipped across the central and southern plains, the skies turned black with dust storms that could last for days and ruined the cropland. A total of 2.5 million people migrated from the Plains region during this time. More than 200,000 of them, known as Okies, migrated to California's agricultural valleys looking for work. This great exodus was the basis for John Steinbeck's classic *The Grapes of Wrath*. During this period, the number of homeless or migratory workers (called hobos) increased dramatically as penniless tramps hopped freight trains hoping to find a better life elsewhere.

Timeline of World War II

JULY 7, 1937: Japan invades China

MARCH 11, 1938: Germany annexes Austria

SEPTEMBER 29, 1938: Munich Pact is signed, forcing the Czechoslovak Republic to cede important military positions to Germany

APRIL 7, 1939: Italy invades Albania

AUGUST 23, 1939: Germany and the Soviet Union sign a non-aggression agreement

SEPTEMBER 1, 1939: Germany invades Poland

SEPTEMBER 3, 1939: Great Britain and France declare war on Germany

APRIL 9, 1940: Beginning of German invasion of Norway and Denmark

JULY 10, 1940: Beginning of the air war known as the Battle of Britain

JUNE 22, 1941: Germany invades Soviet Union

DECEMBER 7, 1941: Japan bombs Pearl Harbor, Hawaii

DECEMBER 8, 1941: United States declares war on Japan

JUNE 1942: Japanese naval forces are defeated at the Battle of Midway

AUGUST-NOVEMBER 1942: United States stops Japanese advance towards Australia at Guadalcanal

OCTOBER 23, 1942: Battle of El Alamein, British rout the German-Italian army in North Africa

NOVEMBER 8, 1942: British and American forces land in French North Africa

SEPTEMBER 9, 1943: American troops land on the beaches of Salerno, Italy

JUNE 4, 1944: Allied troops liberate Rome, Italy

JUNE 6, 1944: American and British troops land at Normandy, France (D-Day)

AUGUST 20, 1944: Allied troops reach Paris, France

OCTOBER 20, 1944: American troops land in the Philippines

DECEMBER 1944: Battle of the Bulge—Germany's last-ditch defense through the Ardennes region of Belgium

MARCH 7, 1945: American troops cross the Rhine River and enter Germany

APRIL 12, 1945: President Franklin Roosevelt dies; Harry S. Truman becomes president

APRIL 28, 1945: Italian partisans capture and execute Benito Mussolini

APRIL 30, 1945: Hitler commits suicide

MAY 7, 1945: Germany surrenders

MAY 8, 1945: V-E Day—Victory in Europe is celebrated

AUGUST 6, 1945: The United States drops an atomic bomb on Hiroshima, Japan

SEPTEMBER 2, 1945: Japan officially surrenders

The Manhattan Project

The first atomic bomb was developed under the code name Manhattan Project, and was a collaborative effort between the United States, Canada and Great Britain. Research and design took place at the secret Los Alamos, New Mexico laboratory. The first nuclear test took place near Alamogordo, New Mexico, code-named "Trinity," on July 16, 1945. Nuclear bombs Little Boy and Fat Man, were dropped on Nagasaki and Hiroshima, Japan in August 1945, bringing a quick end to World War II.

Victims of the Holocaust

It has been estimated that Holocaust victims number between 4.9 and 6 million European Jews and 5 to 10 million people of other groups including:

- Gypsies
- Handicapped persons
- Prisoners of war
- Ethnic Poles
- Soviet civilians
- Homosexuals
- Resistance fighters
- Political prisoners

Rationing

During World War II, ration books and tokens were issued to American families, dictating how much of commodities they could purchase. Rationed items were:

- Tires
- Cars
- Bicycles
- Gasoline
- Sugar
- Coffee
- Meats
- Cheese
- Shoes
- Fuel oil
- Various types of farm equipment

A wartime edition of the *American Woman's Cook Book* advised women to save fat and turn it in at the meat dealer so it could be used for munitions and soap. And because fats were so vital to the war effort, women were encouraged to use them sparingly in cooking.

On the Home Front

Victory gardens—private vegetable and fruit gardens grown to help in the war effort—were just one of the efforts undertaken by the civilian population during World War II. Other civilian support initiatives included the collection of discarded tin cans, a compulsory practice in cities with more than 25,000 people in 1942. Because fat was used in the production of explosives, communities held drives to collect fat and grease produced in everyday cooking. Other drives on the home front included collecting rubber, paper, scrap metal and fur.

Famous People of the Era

FRANKLIN ROOSEVELT (1882-1945): The 32nd president of the United States, elected to four terms of office; died in office on April 12, 1945

HARRY S. TRUMAN (1884-1972): The 33rd President of the United States, vice president under Franklin Roosevelt

GEN. DOUGLAS MACARTHUR (1880-1964): American general best known for his role in the Philippines during World War II

GEN. GEORGE MARSHALL (1880-1959): Army Chief of Staff under FDR

GEN. GEORGE PATTON (1885-1945): Commander of the Seventh Army during the invasion of Sicily in 1943; commanded the Third Army in 1944

DWIGHT D. EISENHOWER (1890-1969): Supreme Allied commander in World War II; coordinated land, sea and air forces for the Normandy landing in 1944

ADM. WILLIAM HALSEY (1882-1959): Naval Commander of the South Pacific Area during the early years of World War II

ADM. CHESTER NIMITZ (1885-1966): Commander in Chief of Pacific Forces during World War II

NEVILLE CHAMBERLAIN (1869-1940): British Prime Minister from 1937-1940, known for his policy of appeasement that allowed Hitler to annex Czechoslovakia

WINSTON CHURCHILL (1874-1965): British Prime Minister, a driving force behind the Allied victory

CHARLES DE GAULLE (1890-1970): French general and statesman, worked with the French resistance, leader of the Free French

JOSEPH STALIN (1879-1953): Second leader of the Soviet Union, his army captured Berlin on May 2, 1945

ERWIN ROMMEL (1891-1944): German Field Marshal, known as the Desert Fox; implicated in a conspiracy to assassinate Adolf Hitler

ADOLF HITLER (1889-1945): Leader of the Nazi party, committed suicide when the Soviet army entered Berlin

BENITO MUSSOLINI (1883-1945): Fascist dictator of Italy from 1922 to 1943

HIROHITO (1901-1989): Emperor of Japan during World War II

ISORUKU YAMAMOTO (1884-1943): Japanese Naval commander during World War II

JOHN DILLINGER (1903-1934): Gangster, bank robber during the Great Depression.

VIVIEN LEIGH (1913-1967): Won Academy Award for Best Actress in 1939 for her role as Scarlett O'Hara in "Gone With the Wind"

CLARK GABLE (1901-1960): Actor, nicknamed "The King of Hollywood;" flew five combat missions during World War II

CLAUDETTE COLBERT (1903-1996): Hollywood star; three of the films she made in 1934 were all nominated for Best Picture

Eleanor Roosevelt

Eleanor Roosevelt was the longest serving First Lady of the United States, spanning 1933 to 1945. With the support of her husband, Mrs. Roosevelt became active in business and politics, holding weekly press conferences and writing a syndicated newspaper column. During World War II, she traveled to the South Pacific, visiting thousands of wounded servicemen. Mrs. Roosevelt was a lifelong supporter of civil rights; in 1941, she visited the Tuskegee Air Corps Advanced Flying School, bringing visibility and legitimacy to the program that trained African-American pilots.

Rosie the Riveter

When the United States entered World War II, the production of war matériel had to increase dramatically. Auto factories were converted to build airplanes and shipyards were expanded to meet the growing need for more naval ships. In an effort to lure more women into the workforce to replace men who had left for the war front, the government launched a campaign centered around the fictional character "Rosie the Riveter." Rosie was depicted as the ideal worker who was loyal, efficient and patriotic.

The campaign attracted minority and lower-class women who were already in the workforce prior to the war. About fifty percent of the women who took war-related jobs were either minority or lower-class. Before the war, women made up a quarter of the U.S. workforce—12 million women—and by the war's end, women made up a third of the workforce (18 million). Following the war, many of the women were forced back into lower-paying jobs.

Inventions of the Era

YEAR	INVENTION
1935	Richter scale
1935	Nylon
1935	Parking meter
1935	Bass guitar
1936	Phillips head screw
1936	Helicopter
1937	Digital computer
1938	Ballpoint pen
1938	Fiberglass
1938	Teflon
1941	Acrylic fiber
1942	Bazooka
1942	SCUBA (self contained underwater breathing apparatus) by Jacques Cousteau
1943	Slinky
1943	Kidney dialysis machine
1945	Atomic bomb

Prices During the Era

YEAR	MILK (PER GALLON)	HOUSE	AVERAGE ANNUAL INCOME
1935	47 cents	$6,296	$1,594
1940	51 cents	$6,558	$1,906
1945	62 cents	$10,131	$2,807

Popular Foods of the Era

- Chicken Sandwich
- Chile Con Carne
- Chicken Gumbo Soup

- Pork and Beans
- Meatloaf
- Bread Pudding
- Stew
- Mashed Potatoes
- Eggless Cake
- Split Pea Soup

Recipes From the Era

Lima Beans and Tomatoes With Bacon

6 pounds dried lima beans
9 quarts water
2 tablespoon salt
2½ pounds sliced bacon
1 no. 10 can tomato puree

Directions:
Wash the beans and soak them overnight in the water. Add the salt and cook until just tender, in the water in which they were soaked. Drain. Cook the bacon until crisp and remove from the fat. Break the bacon into pieces and add with the tomato puree to the beans. Mix well, add more salt if needed, and some of the bacon fat for seasoning. Total measure cooked, about 10¾ quarts; 56 servings, each three-fourths of a cup.

From *Menus and Recipes for Lunches at School* by Clara Rowena Schmidt Carpenter, Helen Rhonda Nebeker Hann, Fanny Walker Yeatman, 1936

Spam and Egg Sandwich

1 tablespoon butter
2 tablespoons chopped onion
1 slice cooked Spam
1 egg, beaten
2 slices bread
1 slice American cheese

Directions:
Melt butter in a small skillet over medium-high heat. Sauté the onion until soft. Mash the Spam, add it to the skillet and cook for 2 or 3 minutes, until browned. Pour the egg into the skillet so that it covers all of the meat and onion. Cook until firm, then flip to brown the other side. Place the egg and meat onto one slice of the bread and top with cheese and tomato (optional). Place the other piece of bread on top.

Songs of the Era

- "As Time Goes By"
- "Boogie Woogie Bugle Boy"
- "Chattanooga Choo Choo"
- "Don't Sit Under the Apple Tree"
- "Goodbye Mama I'm Off to Yokohama"
- "I Left My Heart at The Stage Door Canteen"
- "I'll Be Seeing You"
- "I'll Walk Alone"
- "It's Been a Long, Long Time"
- "Lili Marlene"
- "My Guy's Come Back"
- "A Nightingale Sang in Berkeley Square"
- "Praise the Lord and Pass the Ammunition"
- "Remember Pearl Harbor"
- "Til Then"
- "We'll Meet Again"
- "The White Cliffs of Dover"

Books of the Era

- *Lost Horizon* by James Hilton, 1933
- *Goodbye, Mr. Chips* by James Hilton, 1934
- *For Whom the Bell Tolls* by Ernest Hemingway, 1940
- *Daniel Boone* by James Daugherty (children's book), 1940
- *The Black Stallion* by Walter Farley, 1941
- *Frenchman's Creek* by Daphne du Maurier, 1941

- *The Adventures of Superman* by George Lowther, 1942
- *The Harvey Girls* by Samuel Hopkins Adams, 1942
- *The Little Prince* by Antoine de Saint-Exupéry, 1943
- *The Lady in the Lake* by Raymond Chandler, 1943
- *The Clue in the Jewel Box* by Caroline Keene (Nancy Drew mystery), 1943
- *A Bell for Adano* by John Hersey, 1944
- *Johnny Tremain* by Esther Forbes (children's book), 1944
- *The Age of Reason* by Jean Paul Sartre, 1945
- *The Friendly Persuasion* by Jessamyn West, 1945
- *Cannery Row* by John Steinbeck, 1945

Going to the Movies

YEAR	ACADEMY AWARD FOR BEST FILM	ACADEMY AWARD FOR BEST ACTRESS	ACADEMY AWARD FOR BEST ACTOR
1934	"It Happened One Night"	Claudette Colbert	Clark Gable
1935	"Mutiny on the Bounty"	Bette Davis	Victor McLaglen
1936	"The Great Ziegfeld"	Luise Rainer	Paul Muni
1937	"The Life of Emile Zola"	Luise Rainer	Spencer Tracy
1938	"You Can't Take It With You"	Bette Davis	Spencer Tracy
1939	"Gone With the Wind"	Vivien Leigh	Robert Donat
1940	"Rebecca"	Ginger Rogers	James Stewart
1941	"How Green Was My Valley"	Joan Fontaine	Gary Cooper
1942	"Mrs. Miniver"	Greer Garson	James Cagney
1943	"Casablanca"	Jennifer Jones	Paul Lukas
1944	"Going My Way"	Ingrid Bergman	Bing Crosby
1945	"The Lost Weekend"	Joan Crawford	Ray Milland

10 Most Popular Names 1940–1949

MALE	FEMALE
James	Mary
Robert	Linda
John	Caroline
William	Patricia
Richard	Barbara
David	Jane
Thomas	Judy
Michael	Catherine
Charles	Susan
Joseph	Margaret

Top 10 U.S. Cities by Population in 1940

CITY	POPULATION
New York City	7,454,995
Chicago	3,396,808
Philadelphia	1,931,334
Detroit	1,623,452
Los Angeles	1,504,277
Cleveland	878,336
Baltimore	859,100
St. Louis	816,048
Boston	770,816
Pittsburgh	671,659

Top 10 Immigration by Country 1931–1940

COUNTRY	NUMBER OF IMMIGRANTS
Germany	114,058
Canada/Newfoundland	108,527
Italy	68,028
Mexico	22,319
England	21,756
Poland	17,026
West Indies	15,502
Czechoslovakia	14,393
France	12,623
Ireland	10,973

The U.S. Population Growth 1930–1940

STATE	1930 CENSUS	STATE	1940 CENSUS
New York	12,588,066	New York	13,479,142
Pennsylvania	9,631,350	Pennsylvania	9,900,180
Illinois	7,630,654	Illinois	7,897,241
Ohio	6,646,697	Ohio	6,907,612
Texas	5,824,715	Texas	6,907,387
California	5,677,251	California	6,414,824
Michigan	4,842,325	Michigan	5,256,106
Massachusetts	4,249,614	Massachusetts	4,316,721
New Jersey	4,041,334	New Jersey	4,160,165
Missouri	3,629,367	Missouri	3,784,664
Indiana	3,238,503	North Carolina	3,571,623
North Carolina	3,170,276	Indiana	3,427,796
Wisconsin	2,939,006	Wisconsin	3,137,587

STATE	1930 CENSUS	STATE	1940 CENSUS
Georgia	2,908,506	Georgia	3,123,723
Alabama	2,646,248	Tennessee	2,915,841
Tennessee	2,616,556	Kentucky	2,845,627
Kentucky	2,614,589	Alabama	2,832,961
Minnesota	2,563,953	Minnesota	2,792,300
Iowa	2,470,939	Virginia	2,644,250
Virginia	2,421,851	Iowa	2,538,268
Oklahoma	2,396,040	Louisiana	2,363,880
Louisiana	2,101,593	Oklahoma	2,336,434
Mississippi	2,009,821	Mississippi	2,183,796
Kansas	1,880,999	West Virginia	1,901,974
Arkansas	1,854,482	Arkansas	1,949,387
South Carolina	1,738,765	South Carolina	1,899,804
West Virginia	1,729,205	Florida	1,897,414
Maryland	1,631,526	Maryland	1,821,244
Connecticut	1,606,903	Kansas	1,801,028
Washington	1,563,396	Washington	1,736,191
Florida	1,468,211	Connecticut	1,709,242
Nebraska	1,377,963	Nebraska	1,315,834
Colorado	1,035,791	Colorado	1,123,296
Oregon	953,786	Oregon	1,089,684
Maine	797,423	Maine	847,226
South Dakota	692,849	Rhode Island	713,346
Rhode Island	687,497	District of Columbia	663,091
North Dakota	680,845	South Dakota	642,961
Montana	537,606	North Dakota	641,935
Utah	507,847	Montana	559,456
District of Columbia	486,869	Utah	550,310

STATE	1930 CENSUS	STATE	1940 CENSUS
New Hampshire	465,293	New Mexico	531,818
Idaho	445,032	Idaho	524,873
Arizona	435,573	Arizona	499,261
New Mexico	423,317	New Hampshire	491,524
Vermont	359,611	Vermont	359,231
Delaware	238,380	Delaware	266,505
Wyoming	225,565	Wyoming	250,742
Nevada	91,058	Nevada	110,247

Official Census Dates of the Era

1940: April 1

Non-Population Censuses of the Era

INDIAN RESERVATION CENSUSES: 1885–1940

INDIAN SCHOOL CENSUSES: 1910–1939

Colonial, Territorial and State Censuses of the Era

FLORIDA: 1945

KANSAS: 1941 (veterinarians)

RHODE ISLAND: 1935

SOUTH DAKOTA: 1935, 1945; 1885–1940 (Indian census, various years)

Appendix

U.S. State Fast Facts

STATE	STATEHOOD	PUBLIC OR STATE LAND STATE	FIRST EXTANT U.S. CENSUS	STATEWIDE VITAL RECORDS BEGIN		
				BIRTH	MARRIAGE	DEATH
AL Alabama	1819	Public	1830	1908	1936	1908
AK Alaska	1959	Public	1900	1913	1913	1913
AZ Arizona	1912	Public	1870	1909	1909	1909
AR Arkansas	1836	Public	1830	1914	1917	1914
CA California	1850	Public	1850	1905	1905	1905
CO Colorado	1876	Public	1860 (as four territories), 1870 (as Colorado Territory), 1880 (as a state)	1907	1907	1907
CT Connecticut	1788	State	1790	1897	1897	1897
DE* Delaware	1787	State	1800	1861	1847	1881
FL Florida	1845	Public	1830	1899	1927	1899
GA Georgia	1788	State	1820	1919	1952	1919
HI Hawaii	1959	State	1900	1842	1842	1859
ID Idaho	1890	Public	1850 (as Oregon Territory)	1911	1947	1911

STATE	STATEHOOD	PUBLIC OR STATE LAND STATE	FIRST EXTANT U.S. CENSUS	STATEWIDE VITAL RECORDS BEGIN		
				BIRTH	MARRIAGE	DEATH
IL Illinois	1818	Public	1820	1916	1962	1916
IN Indiana	1816	Public	1820	1907	1958	1899
IA Iowa	1846	Public	1850	1880	1880	1880
KS Kansas	1861	Public	1860	1911	1913	1911
KY Kentucky	1792	State	1810	1911	1958	1911
LA* Louisiana	1812	Public	1810	1914	none	1914
ME Maine	1820	State	1790	892	1892	1892
MD Maryland	1788	State	1790	1898	1950	1898
MA Massachusetts	1788	State	1790	1841	1841	1841
MI Michigan	1837	Public	1820	1867	1867	1867
MN Minnesota	1858	Public	1820 (in Michigan Territory)	1900	1958	1908
MS Mississippi	1817	Public	1820	1912	1926	1912
MO Missouri	1821	Public	1830	1910	1881	1910

STATE	STATEHOOD	PUBLIC OR STATE LAND STATE	FIRST EXTANT U.S. CENSUS	STATEWIDE VITAL RECORDS BEGIN		
				BIRTH	MARRIAGE	DEATH
MT Montana	1889	Public	1870	1907	1943	1907
NE Nebraska	1867	Public	1860	1905	1909	1905
NV Nevada	1864	Public	1850	1911	1968	1911
NH New Hampshire	1788	State	1790	1901	1901	1901
NJ New Jersey	1787	State	1830 (Cumberland County only in 1800)	1848	1848	1848
NM New Mexico	1912	Public	1850	1920	1920	1920
NY New York	1788	State	1790	1880	1880	1880
NC North Carolina	1789	State	1790	1913	1962	1913
ND North Dakota	1889	Public	1900	1907	1925	1907
OH Ohio	1803	Public	1820 (Washington County only in 1810)	1908	1949	1908
OK Oklahoma	1907	Public	1860	1908	1908	1908
OR Oregon	1859	Public	1850	1903	1906	1903
PA Pennsylvania	1787	State	1798	1906	1885	1906

STATE	STATEHOOD	PUBLIC OR STATE LAND STATE	FIRST EXTANT U.S. CENSUS	STATEWIDE VITAL RECORDS BEGIN		
				BIRTH	MARRIAGE	DEATH
RI Rhode Island	1790	State	1790	1853	1853	1853
SC South Carolina	1788	State	1790	1915	1950	1915
SD South Dakota	1889	Public	1900	1905	1905	1905
TN* Tennessee	1796	State	1830	1908	1945	1908
TX* Texas	1845	State	1850	1903	1966	1903
UT Utah	1896	Public	1850	1905	1887	1905
VT Vermont	1791	State	1790	1955	1955	1955
VA Virginia	1788	State	1810 (partial)	1912	1912	1912
WA Washington	1889	Public	1860	1907	1968	1907
WV West Virginia	1863	State	1870 (earlier censuses as part of Virginia)	1917	1964	1917
WI Wisconsin	1848	Public	1820	1907	1907	1907
WY Wyoming	1890	Public	1870	1909	1941	1909

**Delaware's statewide birth and death records stop in 1863 and resume in 1881. Louisiana birth records are kept in parish clerk offices. Tennessee has no statewide birth or death records for 1913. Texas was established as the Republic of Texas (not a territory) in 1836.*

War Records to Search For

Learn which military records to search for based on your ancestors' birth dates.

IF AN ANCESTOR WAS BORN IN ...	LOOK FOR RECORDS OF THE ...
1726-1767	Revolutionary War (1775-1783)
1762-1799	War of 1812 (1812-1815)
1796-1831	Mexican-American War (1846-1848)
1811-1848	Civil War (1861-1865)
1848-1881	Spanish-American War (1898)
1849-1885	Philippine Insurrection (1899-1902)
1872-1900	World War I (1917-1918)
1877-1925	World War II (1941-1945)
1900-1936	Korean War (1950-1953)
1914-1955	Vietnam War (early 1960s-1973)

Major Genealogical Records Generated from U.S. Wars

Depending on the war in which your ancestor served, you'll find a variety of types of military records.

WAR	SERVICE RECORDS/ MUSTER ROLLS	PENSION RECORDS	BOUNTY-LAND WARRANTS	DRAFT CARDS
Colonial Wars	X		X	
Revolutionary War	X	X	X	
War of 1812	X	X	X	
Mexican-American War	X	X	X	
Civil War	X	X		
Spanish-American War	X			
World War I	X			X
World War II	X			X
Korean War	X			
Vietnam War	X			

U.S. Immigrants by Country (1820 to 1975)

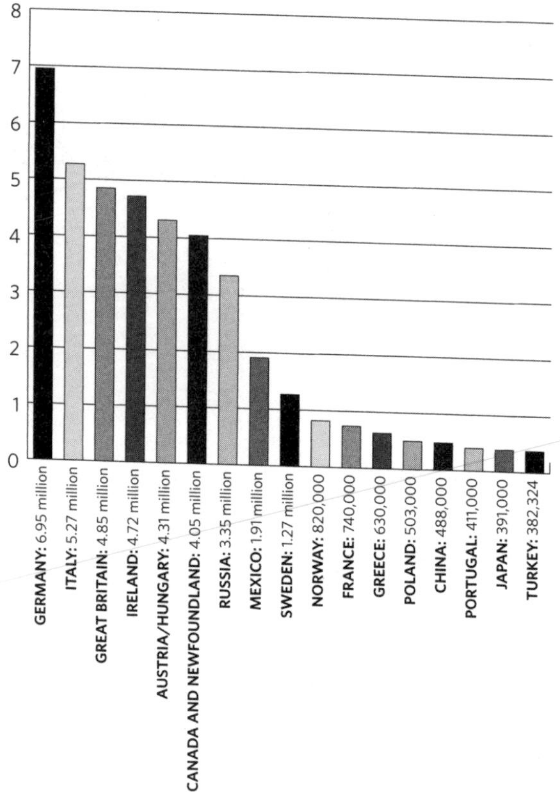
8
7
6
5
4
3
2
1
0
GERMANY: 6.95 million
ITALY: 5.27 million
GREAT BRITAIN: 4.85 million
IRELAND: 4.72 million
AUSTRIA/HUNGARY: 4.31 million
CANADA AND NEWFOUNDLAND: 4.05 million
RUSSIA: 3.35 million
MEXICO: 1.91 million
SWEDEN: 1.27 million
NORWAY: 820,000
FRANCE: 740,000
GREECE: 630,000
POLAND: 503,000
CHINA: 488,000
PORTUGAL: 411,000
JAPAN: 391,000
TURKEY: 382,324

Timeline of Immigration Laws

1790 The United States establishes uniform naturalization rules for white males 21 and older; children of naturalized citizens get automatic citizenship.

1795 Free white females age 21 and older can become citizens.

1804 Widows and children can become citizens if the husband or father died before filing final papers.

1824 Alien minors, upon turning 21, can be naturalized if they've lived in the United States for five years.

1855 Alien women become citizens upon marrying U.S. citizens.

1862 Aliens who have received honorable discharges from the U.S. Army can skip filing declarations of intention.

1868 14th Amendment declares former slaves citizens.

1870 People of African descent may become citizens.

1882 Chinese Exclusion Act passes.

1887 Dawes Act entitles American Indians who have accepted land allotments to become citizens.

1891 Bureau of Immigration is established.

1894 Declaration of intention waived for aliens who are honorably discharged after five years in the Navy or Marine Corps.

1906 Bureau of Immigration and Naturalization Service (INS) is established.

1917 Puerto Ricans become U.S. citizens.

1922 Married women's citizenship becomes independent of their husbands'.

1924 American Indians are granted full citizenship; quotas severely reduce immigration.

1929 Photographs are required on petition for naturalization.

1940 Alien Registration Act required non-naturalized aliens to register with the government.

1943 Asian immigrants can become citizens.

1952 Age requirement for naturalization drops to 18; declaration of intention becomes optional.

1990 Courts no longer naturalize citizens.

2003 INS becomes U.S. Citizenship and Immigration Services.

Major U.S. Migration Routes

BRADDOCK'S ROAD: New York and Pennsylvania
This route connected Cumberland, Maryland, on the Potomac River to the Monongahela River south of present-day Pittsburgh. In 1813, construction began on the Cumberland Road (later, the National Road), which followed much the same route.

CALIFORNIA TRAIL: Utah, California, Oregon, Washington
Blazed in 1841, this trail split off of the Oregon Trail at Soda Springs, Idaho, after Fort Bridger. It followed the Bear River and crossed the Great Salt Lake Desert and Sierra Nevadas.

CALIFORNIA GOLD RUSH MIGRANTS TRIED OTHER ROUTES:
Some went north of the Great Salt Lake and through a corner of Idaho to rejoin the trail at the Humboldt River. From Nevada, the Lassen Route aimed north of Sutter's Mill, while the southerly Carson Route headed southwest.

CAROLINA ROAD: Virginia, the Carolinas and Georgia
An alternative to the Fall Line Road, the Carolina Road (also called the Upper Road) tracked through Hillsboro and Charlotte, North Carolina, in the 1750s. It originally extended to Greenville, South Carolina, but in 1828 connected to the Federal Road at Athens, Georgia.

CHICAGO ROAD: Northwest Territory
This crude road from Detroit to Chicago, built between 1829 and 1836, brought pioneers to southern Michigan and Illinois.

DE ANZA TRAIL: Arizona, Utah, California, Oregon, Washington
In 1776, Spanish Lt. Col. Juan Bautista de Anza led almost 300 people over 1,200 miles to settle Alta (Upper) California. The first overland route connecting New Spain with San Francisco, the U.S. segment begins at Nogales, Arizona.

***EL CAMINO REAL DE LOS TEJAS*: Southwest**
During the Spanish colonial period, this was the primary overland trail from what's now Mexico, across the Rio Grande to east Texas and the Red River Valley in what's now northwest Louisiana.

***EL CAMINO REAL DE TIERRA ADENTRO*: Southwest**
This north-south route connected Mexico City with what's now northern New Mexico. Its U.S. section stretches from El Paso, Texas, to San Juan Pueblo, New Mexico.

FALL LINE ROAD: Virginia, the Carolinas and Georgia
Beginning in about 1735, travelers would leave King's Highway at Fredericksburg, Virginia, and head southwest to Augusta, Georgia, at the head of the Savannah River. Eventually, many Alabama- and Mississippi-bound pioneers would follow the Fall Line Road to link up with the new Federal Road in Columbus, Georgia.

FEDERAL ROAD: Alabama, Mississippi, Louisiana and Texas
In 1806 Congress appropriated $6,400 for this road to carry mail between Athens, Georgia, and New Orleans. It was widened and partly rerouted in 1811; connecting Fort Stoddert, Alabama (north of Mobile), to Fort Wilkinson, Georgia, on the Chattahoochee River, where the route merged with the original postal path.

GREAT VALLEY ROAD: Virginia, the Carolinas and Georgia
Known to Indians as the Great Warrior Path, this trail's forerunner reached from New York to present-day Salisbury, North Carolina, where it connected with the Great Trading Path. Its feeders included the Philadelphia Wagon Road, which in the 1740s, linked up with the Pioneer's Road from Alexandria, Virginia, and went on to Winchester, Virginia The Great Valley Road also became a feeder into the Wilderness Road.

KING'S HIGHWAY: Virginia, the Carolinas and Georgia

Incorporating the Boston Post Road between Boston and New York, King's Highway could be called America's first interstate. It eventually stretched 1,300 miles south from Boston through most of the Colonies' important cities, to Charleston, South Carolina.

MOHAWK TRAIL: New York and Pennsylvania

By 1770, this trail reached from Albany to Buffalo. The Catskill Turnpike overlapped it after the Revolutionary War. In 1825, the Erie Canal provided a waterway from Albany to Lake Erie.

MORMON TRAIL: Utah, California, Oregon, Washington

Mormon leader Brigham Young set off with his followers from Nauvoo, Illinois, in 1846. They crossed Iowa and the Missouri River to the site of present-day Florence, Nebraska, then traced the north bank of the Platte River from Fort Kearny, Nebraska, to Fort Laramie, Wyoming, where they turned southwest to Salt Lake City.

NATCHEZ TRACE: Tennessee, Mississippi, Louisiana

The first major north-south route in the South, the Natchez Trace followed Indian trails from Nashville, Tennessee, to Natchez, Mississippi, on the Mississippi River. The 500-mile route was upgraded in 1806, and briefly supplanted by the Jackson Military Road, which reached New Orleans in 1820.

NATIONAL ROAD: Northwest Territory

Originally the Cumberland Road, the route was called the National Road by 1825 because of its Congressional funding. Construction of the 600-mile span, which eventually stretched from Cumberland, Maryland, (incorporating the old Braddock's Road) to Vandalia, Illinois, began in 1811.

OLD SPANISH TRAIL: Southwest

This trail and its variants connected Santa Fe and Los Angeles, key outposts of what was then Mexico, from 1829 to 1848. The 2,700-mile trail crossed deserts, canyons and Death Valley.

OREGON TRAIL: Utah, California, Oregon, Washington

The Oregon Trail covered 2,000 miles in seven states. It stretched from Independence, Missouri, to Fort Kearny, followed the south bank of the Platte River, crossed Wyoming to Fort Bridger and turned northwest through what's now Idaho. At The Dalles, Oregon, migrants took the Columbia River or, after 1846, the safer but longer Barlow toll road across the Cascade Range to the Willamette Valley.

PENNSYLVANIA ROAD: New York and Pennsylvania

Incorporating the Great Conestoga Road and then later Lancaster Pike, the Pennsylvania Road connected Philadelphia to Pittsburgh. Much of the route west of Harrisburg followed the early path of Forbes Road.

RICHMOND ROAD: Kentucky and Tennessee

Many settlers bound for Kentucky traveled this route through Virginia from Richmond to Fort Chiswell, where it joined the Great Valley Road.

SANTA FE TRAIL: Southwest

More a commercial route than a migration path, this famous trail also was traveled by gold seekers and by American troops in the war with Mexico from 1821 until the railroad arrived in 1880. The 1,200-mile route crossed five states, from Franklin, Missouri, to Santa Fe, New Mexico.

STATE ROAD: Northwest Territory

Connecting to the Chicago Road, the State Road extended west from Chicago through Elgin and Rockford to Galena, Illinois, on the Mississippi River.

WILDERNESS ROAD: Kentucky and Tennessee

Daniel Boone led six families through the Cumberland Gap into Kentucky in 1775, pathfinding what was originally called Boone's Trace but would become known as the Wilderness Road when it was widened in 1796. Tennessee-bound settlers took the Knoxville Road south from Kentucky to the Nashville Road, or the Nickajack Trail from Fort Loudon (now in Tennessee) to the Chickasaw Trail (later renamed Robert's Road).

ZANE'S TRACE: Northwest Territory

In 1796 and 1797, Col. Ebenezer Zane built this road through Ohio between Wheeling, West Virginia, and Maysville, Kentucky. The segment between Wheeling and Zanesville, Ohio, also called the Wheeling Road, was ultimately upgraded and incorporated into the National Road.

Dedication

This book is dedicated to my sister, Vicki. Her love of history has taken her to some of the most significant historic destinations in America. She truly has seen it all, from sea-to-shining sea.

About the Author

Nancy Hendrickson is the author of *Discover Your Family History Online*, *Remembering Old California*, *Events This Day in History* and *San Diego Then and Now*. Learn more about her genealogy coaching at AncestorNews.com. Nancy lives in San Diego, Calif., and is an enthusiastic digital photographer and historical traveler.

 Published by Family Tree Books, an imprint of F+W Media, Inc., 10151 Carver Road, Suite 200, Blue Ash, Ohio 45242. (800) 289-0963. First edition.

For more genealogy resources, visit
<shopfamilytree.com>.

17 16 15 14 5 4 3

ISBN: 978-1-4403-2527-4

Distributed in Canada by Fraser Direct
100 Armstrong Ave.
Georgetown, Ontario, Canada L7G 5S4
Tel: (905) 877-4411

Distributed in the U.K. and Europe by F&W Media International, LTD
Brunel House, Forde Close, Newton Abbot, TQ12 4PU, UK
Tel: (+44) 1626 323200
Fax: (+44) 1626 323319
E-mail: enquiries@fwmedia.com

Distributed in Australia by Capricorn Link
PO Box 704, Windsor, NSW 2756 Australia
Tel: (02) 4560-1600
Fax: (02) 4577-5288
E-mail: books@capricornlink.com.au

PUBLISHER/ EDITORIAL DIRECTOR
Allison Dolan

EDITED BY
Jacqueline Musser

DESIGNED BY
Julie Barnett

PRODUCTION COORDINATED BY
Debbie Thomas